This book is presented

to

Mary Ann Kane

By the Board of Education of the
School District of

Absecon, N. J.

Upon completion of Grade Eight
in the Public Schools

H. A. Marsh Principal

Absecon School

Ralph Bartlett Superintendent
Pres. Board of Education

Date *June 6, 1945*

THE LIBERTY BELL'S FIRST NOTE—1753

OUR
GREAT STATE PAPERS

THE DECLARATION OF INDEPENDENCE

THE CONSTITUTION OF THE UNITED STATES

THE CONSTITUTION OF NEW JERSEY

THE HISTORY OF AND PLEDGE TO THE UNITED STATES FLAG

THE JOHN C. WINSTON COMPANY

CHICAGO
ATLANTA

PHILADELPHIA

LOS ANGELES
DALLAS

CONTENTS

THE AMERICAN'S CREED

I believe in the United States of America as a government of the people, by the people, for the people; whose just powers are derived from the consent of the governed; a democracy in a republic; a sovereign nation of many sovereign states; a perfect Union, one and inseparable; established upon those principles of freedom, equality, justice, and humanity for which American patriots sacrificed their lives and fortunes.

I therefore believe it is my duty to my country to love it, to support its Constitution, to obey its laws, to respect its flag, and to defend it against all enemies.

—*William Tyler Page.*

THE DECLARATION OF INDEPENDENCE

THE DECLARATION OF INDEPENDENCE

In Congress July 4, 1776

The Unanimous Declaration of the Thirteen United States of America

When in the course of human events, it becomes necessary for one people to dissolve the political bands which have connected them with another, and to assume among the powers of the earth, the separate and equal station to which the Laws of Nature and of Nature's God entitles them, a decent respect to the opinions of mankind requires that they should declare the causes which impel them to the separation.

We hold these truths to be self-evident, that all men are created equal, that they are endowed by their Creator with certain unalienable Rights, that among these are Life, Liberty and the pursuit of Happiness. That to secure these rights, Governments are instituted among Men, deriving their just powers from the consent of the governed. That whenever any Form of Government becomes destructive of these ends, it is the Right of the People to alter or to abolish it, and to institute new Government, laying its foundation on such principles and organizing its powers in such form, as to them shall seem most likely to effect their Safety and Happiness. Prudence, indeed, will dictate that Governments long established should not be changed for light and transient causes; and accordingly all experience hath shewn, that mankind are more disposed to suffer, while evils are sufferable, than to right themselves by abolishing the forms to which they are accustomed. But when a long train of abuses and usurpations, pursuing invariably the same Object, evinces a design to reduce them under absolute Despotism, it is their right, it is their duty, to throw off such Government, and to provide new Guards for their future security. Such has been the patient sufferance of these Colonies; and such is now the necessity which constrains them to alter their former Systems of Government. The history of the present King of Great Britain is a history of repeated injuries and usurpations, all having in direct object the establishment of an absolute Tyranny over these States. To prove this, let Facts be submitted to a candid world.

He has refused his Assent to Laws, the most wholesome and necessary for the public good.

He has forbidden his Governors to pass Laws of immediate and pressing importance, unless suspended in their operation till his Assent should be obtained; and when so suspended, he has utterly neglected to attend to them.

He has refused to pass other Laws for the accommodation of large districts of people, unless those people would relinquish the right of Representation in the Legislature, a right inestimable to them and formidable to tyrants only.

He has called together legislative bodies at places unusual, uncomfortable, and distant from the depository of their public Records, for the sole purpose of fatiguing them into compliance with his measures.

He has dissolved Representative Houses repeatedly, for opposing with manly firmness his invasions on the rights of the people.

He has refused for a long time, after such dissolutions, to cause others to be elected; whereby the Legislative powers, incapable of Annihilation, have returned to the People at large for their exercise; the State remaining in the meantime exposed to all the dangers of invasion from without, and convulsions within.

He has endeavored to prevent the population of these States; for that purpose obstructing the Laws for Naturalization of Foreigners; refusing to pass others to encourage their migrations hither, and raising the conditions of new Appropriations of Lands.

He has obstructed the Administration of Justice, by refusing his Assent to Laws for establishing Judiciary Powers.

He has made Judges dependent on his Will alone, for the tenure of their offices, and the amount and payment of their salaries.

He has erected a multitude of New Offices, and sent hither swarms of Officers to harass our people, and eat out their substance.

He has kept among us, in times of peace, Standing Armies without the Consent of our legislature.

He has affected to render the Military independent of and superior to the Civil power.

He has combined with others to subject us to a jurisdiction foreign to our constitution, and unacknowledged by our loss; giving his Assent to their Acts of pretended Legislation:

For quartering large bodies of armed troops among us:

For protecting them, by a mock Trial, from punishment for any Murders which they should commit on the Inhabitants of these States:

For cutting off our Trade with all parts of the world:

For imposing Taxes on us without our Consent:

For depriving us in many cases of the benefits of Trial by jury:

For transporting us beyond Seas to be tried for pretended offences:

For abolishing the free System of English Laws in a neighboring Province, establishing therein an Arbitrary government, and enlarging its Boundaries so as to render it at once an example and fit instrument for introducing the same absolute rule into these Colonies:

For taking away our Charters, abolishing our most valuable Laws, and altering fundamentally the Forms of our Governments:

For suspending our own Legislatures, and declaring themselves invested with power to legislate for us in all cases whatsoever.

He has abdicated Government here, by declaring us out of his Protection and waging war against us.

He has plundered our seas, ravaged our Coasts, burnt our towns, and destroyed the lives of our people.

He is at this time transporting large Armies of foreign Mercenaries to complete the works of death, desolation and tyranny, already begun with circumstances of Cruelty and perfidy scarcely paralleled in the most barbarous ages, and totally unworthy the Head of a civilized nation.

N J

He has constrained our fellow-Citizens taken captive on the high Seas to bear Arms against their Country, to become the executioners of their friends and Brethren, or to fall themselves by their Hands.

He has excited domestic insurrections amongst us, and has endeavored to bring on the inhabitants of our frontiers, the merciless Indian Savages, whose known rule of warfare is an undistinguished destruction of all ages, sexes and conditions.

In every stage of these Oppressions We have Petitioned for Redress in the most humble terms. Our repeated Petitions have been answered only by repeated injury. A Prince, whose character is thus Marked by every act which may define a Tyrant, is unfit to be the ruler of a free people.

Nor have We been wanting in attentions to our British brethren. We have warned them from time to time of attempts by their legislature to extend an unwarrantable jurisdiction over us. We have reminded them of the circumstances of our emigration and settlement here. We have appealed to their native justice and magnanimity, and we have conjured them by the ties of our common kindred to disavow these usurpations, which would inevitably interrupt our connections and correspondence. They too have been deaf to the voice of justice and of consanguinity. We must therefore, acquiesce in the necessity which denounces our Separation, and hold them, as we hold the rest of mankind, Enemies in War, in Peace Friends.

WE, THEREFORE, the REPRESENTATIVES of the UNITED STATES OF AMERICA, IN GENERAL CONGRESS, Assembled, appealing to the Supreme Judge of the world for the rectitude of our intentions, do, in the Name, and by the authority of the good People of these Colonies, solemnly PUBLISH and DECLARE, That these United Colonies are, and of Right ought to be FREE AND INDEPENDENT States; that they are Absolved from all Allegiance to the British Crown, and that all political connection between them and the State of Great Britain, is and ought to be totally dissolved; and that as FREE AND INDEPENDENT STATES, they have full Power to levy War, conclude Peace, contract Alliances, establish Commerce, and to do all other Acts and Things which

Independent States may of right do. And for the support of this Declaration, with a firm reliance on the protection of Divine Providence, We mutually pledge to each other our Lives, our Fortunes, and our sacred Honor.

SIGNERS OF THE DECLARATION OF INDEPENDENCE

Name	Colony	Occupation	Born	Birthplace	Died	Age
Adams, John	Mass..	Lawyer....	1735	Braintree, Mass........	1826	92
Adams, Samuel	Mass..	Merchant..	1722	Boston, Mass...........	1803	81
Bartlett, Josiah	N. H..	Physician..	1729	Amesbury, Mass........	1795	67
Braxton, Carter	Va...	Planter....	1736	Newington, Va..........	1797	62
Carroll, Charles	Md...	Lawyer....	1737	Annapolis, Md..........	1832	96
Chase, Samuel	Md...	Lawyer....	1741	Somerset Co., Md.......	1811	71
Clark, Abraham	N.J...	Lawyer....	1726	Elizabethtown, N. J.....	1794	69
Clymer, George	Pa....	Merchant..	1739	Philadelphia, Pa........	1813	75
Ellery, William	R. I...	Lawyer....	1727	Newport, R. I..........	1820	93
Floyd, William	N. Y...	Farmer....	1734	Setauket, N. Y.........	1821	87
Franklin, Benjamin	Pa....	Printer....	1706	Boston, Mass...........	1790	85
Gerry, Elbridge	Mass..	Merchant..	1744	Marblehead, Mass......	1814	71
Gwinnett, Button	Ga....	Merchant..	1732	England..............	1777	45
Hancock, John	Mass..	Merchant..	1737	Braintree, Mass........	1793	57
Hall, Lyman	Ga....	Physician..	1731	Connecticut...........	1784	53
Harrison, Benjamin	Va....	Farmer....	1740	Berkeley, Va...........	1791	51
Hart, John	N.J...	Farmer....	1715	Hopewell, N. J.........	1780	65
Hewes, Joseph	N. C...	Lawyer....	1730	Kingston, N. J.........	1779	49
Heyward, Thomas, Jr..	S. C...	Lawyer....	1746	St. Luke's, S. C........	1809	63
Hooper, William	N. C...	Lawyer....	1742	Boston, Mass..........	1790	49
Hopkins, Stephen	R. I...	Farmer....	1707	Scituate, Mass.........	1785	79
Hopkinson, Francis	N.J...	Lawyer....	1737	Philadelphia, Pa........	1791	54
Huntington, Samuel	Conn..	Lawyer....	1732	Windham, Conn........	1796	64
Jefferson, Thomas	Va....	Lawyer....	1743	Shadwell, Va...........	1826	83
Lee, Richard Henry	Va....	Soldier....	1732	Stratford, Va..........	1794	63
Lee, Francis Lightfoot..	Va....	Farmer....	1734	Stratford, Va..........	1797	63
Lewis, Francis	N. Y...	Merchant..	1713	Llandaff, Wales........	1803	91
Livingston, Philip	N. Y...	Merchant..	1716	Albany, N. Y..........	1778	63
Lynch, Thomas, Jr	S. C...	Lawyer....	1749	Prince George's Co., S. C.	1779	30
McKean, Thomas	Del...	Lawyer....	1734	New London, Pa.......	1817	84
Middleton, Arthur	S. C...	Lawyer....	1743	Middleton Pl., S. C.....	1788	44
Morris, Lewis	N. Y...	Farmer....	1726	Morrisania, N. Y.......	1798	72
Morris, Robert	Pa....	Merchant..	1734	Lancashire, England....	1806	73
Morton, John	Pa....	Surveyor..	1724	Ridley, Pa.............	1777	53
Nelson, Thomas, Jr....	Va....	Statesman..	1738	York, Va..............	1789	51
Paca, William	Md...	Lawyer....	1740	Wye Hall, Md..........	1799	59
Paine, Robert Treat....	Mass..	Lawyer....	1731	Boston, Mass..........	1814	84
Penn, John	N. C...	Lawyer....	1741	Caroline Co., Va.......	1788	48
Read, George	Del...	Lawyer....	1734	Cecil Co., Md..........	1798	64
Rodney, Cæsar	Del...	General....	1730	Dover, Del............	1783	53
Ross, George	Pa....	Lawyer....	1730	New Castle, Del........	1779	49
Rush, Benjamin	Pa....	Physician..	1745	Berberry, Pa...........	1813	68
Rutledge, Edward	S. C..	Lawyer....	1749	Charleston, S. C........	1800	51
Sherman, Roger	Conn..	Shoemaker.	1721	Newton, Mass.........	1793	73
Smith, James	Pa....	Lawyer....	1710	Ireland..............	1806	96
Stockton, Richard	N.J...	Lawyer....	1730	Princeton, N. J........	1781	51
Stone, Thomas	Md...	Lawyer....	1742	Pointoin Manor, Md....	1787	45
Taylor, George	Pa....	Physician..	1716	Ireland..............	1781	65
Thornton, Matthew	N. H..	Physician..	1714	Ireland..............	1803	89
Walton, George	Ga....	Lawyer....	1740	Frederick Co., Va.......	1804	64
Whipple, William	Conn..	Sailor....	1730	Kittery, Me...........	1785	55
Williams, William	Conn..	Statesman..	1731	Lebanon, Conn........	1811	81
Wilson, James	Pa....	Lawyer....	1742	St. Andrews, Scotland..	1798	56
Witherspoon, John	N.J...	Minister..	1722	Yester, Scotland.......	1794	73
Wolcott, Oliver	Conn..	Physician..	1726	Windsor, Conn.........	1797	72
Wythe, George	Va....	Lawyer....	1726	Elizabeth Co., Va.......	1806	80

N J

THE CONSTITUTION
OF THE UNITED STATES

We hold these truths to be self-evident,—that all men are created equal; that they are endowed by their Creator with certain inalienable rights; that among these are Life, Liberty, and the pursuit of happiness.

THOMAS JEFFERSON—*Declaration of Independence of the United States of America.*

THE CONSTITUTION
OF THE UNITED STATES

Preamble.—We, the people of the United States, in order to form a more perfect Union, establish justice, insure domestic tranquillity, provide for the common defence, promote the general welfare, and secure the blessings of liberty to ourselves and our posterity, do ordain and establish this CONSTITUTION for the United States of America.

ARTICLE I

Legislative Powers.—SECTION I.   All legislative powers herein granted shall be vested in a Congress of the United States, which shall consist of a Senate and House of Representatives.

House of Representatives.—SECTION II.   1. The House of Representatives shall be composed of members chosen every second year by the people of the several States, and the electors in each State shall have the qualifications requisite for electors of the most numerous branch of the State Legislature.

Qualifications of Representatives.—2. No person shall be a Representative who shall not have attained to the age of twenty-five years, and been seven years a citizen of the United States, and who shall not, when elected, be an inhabitant of that State in which he shall be chosen.

Apportionment of Representatives.—3. Representatives and direct taxes shall be apportioned among the several States which may be included within this Union according to their respective numbers, which shall be determined by adding to the whole number of free persons, including those bound to service for a term of years, and excluding Indians not taxed, three-fifths of all other persons.   The actual enumeration shall be made within three years after the first meeting of the Congress of the United States, and within every subsequent term of ten years, in such manner as they shall by law direct.   The number of Representatives shall not exceed one for every thirty thousand, but each State shall have at least one Representative;   and until such enumeration shall be made the State of New Hampshire shall be entitled to choose 3; Massachusetts, 8; Rhode Island and Providence Plantations, 1; Connecticut, 5; New York, 6; New Jersey,

4; Pennsylvania, 8; Delaware, 1; Maryland, 6; Virginia, 10; North Carolina, 5; South Carolina, 5; and Georgia, 3.*

Vacancies, How Filled.—4. When vacancies happen in the representation from any State, the Executive Authority thereof shall issue writs of election to fill such vacancies.

Officers, How Appointed.—5. The House of Representatives shall choose their Speaker and other officers, and shall have the sole power of impeachment.

Senate.—SECTION III. 1. The Senate of the United States shall be composed of two Senators from each State, chosen by the Legislature thereof, for six years; and each Senator shall have one vote.†

Classification of Senators.—2. Immediately after they shall be assembled in consequence of the first election, they shall be divided as equally as may be into three classes. The seats of the Senators of the first class shall be vacated at the expiration of the second year, of the second class at the expiration of the fourth year, and of the third class at the expiration of the sixth year, so that one-third may be chosen every second year; and if vacancies happen by resignation, or otherwise, during the recess of the Legislature of any State, the Executive thereof may make temporary appointments until the next meeting of the Legislature, which shall then fill such vacancies.

Qualifications of Senators.—3. No person shall be a Senator who shall not have attained to the age of thirty years, and been nine years a citizen of the United States, and who shall not, when elected, be an inhabitant of that State for which he shall be chosen.

President of the Senate.—4. The Vice-President of the United States shall be President of the Senate, but shall have no vote unless they be equally divided.

5. The Senate shall choose their other officers, and also a President pro tempore, in the absence of the Vice-President, or when he shall exercise the office of President of the United States.

Senate a Court for Trial of Impeachments.—6. The Senate shall have the sole power to try all impeachments. When sitting for that purpose, they shall be on oath or affirmation. When

* See Article XIV, Amendments.
† See Article XVII, Amendments.

the President of the United States is tried, the Chief Justice shall preside; and no person shall be convicted without the concurrence of two-thirds of the members present.

Judgment in Case of Conviction.—7. Judgment in cases of impeachment shall not extend further than to removal from office, and disqualification to hold and enjoy any office of honor, trust, or profit under the United States; but the party convicted shall nevertheless be liable and subject to indictment, trial, judgment, and punishment, according to law.

Elections of Senators and Representatives.—Section IV. 1. The times, places, and manner of holding elections for Senators and Representatives shall be prescribed in each State by the Legislature thereof; but the Congress may at any time by law make or alter such regulations, except as to places of choosing Senators.

Meeting of Congress.—2. The Congress shall assemble at least once in every year, and such meeting shall be on the first Monday in December, unless they shall by law appoint a different day.

Organization of Congress.—Section V. 1. Each House shall be the judge of the elections, returns, and qualifications of its own members, and a majority of each shall constitute a quorum to do business; but a smaller number may adjourn from day to day, and may be authorized to compel the attendance of absent members in such manner and under such penalties as each House may provide.

Rule of Proceedings.—2. Each House may determine the rules of its proceedings, punish its members for disorderly behavior, and with the concurrence of two-thirds expel a member.

Journals of Each House.—3. Each House shall keep a journal of its proceedings, and from time to time publish the same, excepting such parts as may in their judgment require secrecy; and the yeas and nays of the members of either House on any question shall, at the desire of one-fifth of those present, be entered on the journal.

Adjournment of Congress.—4. Neither House, during the session of Congress, shall, without the consent of the other, adjourn for more than three days, nor to any other place than that in which the two Houses shall be sitting.

Pay and Privileges of Members.—SECTION VI. 1. The Senators and Representatives shall receive a compensation for their services, to be ascertained by law, and paid out of the Treasury of the United States. They shall in all cases, except treason, felony, and breach of the peace, be privileged from arrest during their attendance at the session of their respective Houses, and in going to and returning from the same; and for any speech or debate in either House they shall not be questioned in any other place.

Other Offices Prohibited.—2. No Senator or Representative shall, during the time for which he was elected, be appointed to any civil office under the authority of the United States which shall have been created, or the emoluments whereof shall have been increased during such time; and no person holding any office under the United States shall be a member of either House during his continuance in office.

Revenue Bills.—SECTION VII. 1. All bills for raising revenue shall originate in the House of Representatives, but the Senate may propose or concur with amendments, as on other bills.

How Bills Become Laws.—2. Every bill which shall have passed the House of Representatives and the Senate shall, before it become a law, be presented to the President of the United States; if he approve, he shall sign it, but if not, he shall return it, with his objections, to that House in which it shall have originated, who shall enter the objections at large on their journal, and proceed to reconsider it. If after such reconsideration two-thirds of that House shall agree to pass the bill, it shall be sent, together with the objections, to the other House, by which it shall likewise be reconsidered; and if approved by two-thirds of that House it shall become a law. But in all such cases the votes of both Houses shall be determined by yeas and nays and the names of the persons voting for and against the bill shall be entered on the journal of each House respectively. If any bill shall not be returned by the President within ten days (Sundays excepted) after it shall have been presented to him, the same shall be a law, in like manner as if he had signed it, unless the Congress by their adjournment prevent its return; in which case it shall not be a law.

Approval and Veto Powers of the President.—3. Every order, resolution, or vote to which the concurrence of the Senate and House of Representatives may be necessary (except on a question of adjournment) shall be presented to the President of the United States; and before the same shall take effect shall be approved by him, or, being disapproved by him, shall be repassed by two-thirds of the Senate and the House of Representatives, according to the rules and limitations prescribed in the case of a bill.

Powers Vested in Congress.—SECTION VIII. 1. The Congress shall have power:

To lay and collect taxes, duties, imposts, and excises, to pay the debts and provide for the common defence and general welfare of the United States; but all duties, imposts, and excises shall be uniform throughout the United States.

2. To borrow money on the credit of the United States.

3. To regulate commerce with foreign nations, and among the several States, and with the Indian tribes.

4. To establish an uniform rule of naturalization, and uniform laws on the subject of bankruptcies throughout the United States.

5. To coin money, regulate the value thereof, and of foreign coin, and fix the standard of weights and measures.

6. To provide for the punishment of counterfeiting the securities and current coin of the United States.

7. To establish post offices and post roads.

8. To promote the progress of science and useful arts by securing for limited times to authors and inventors the exclusive rights to their respective writings and discoveries.

9. To constitute tribunals inferior to the Supreme Court.

10. To define and punish piracies and felonies committed on the high seas, and offences against the law of nations.

11. To declare war, grant letters of marque and reprisal, and make rules concerning captures on land and water.

12. To raise and support armies, but no appropriation of money to that use shall be for a longer term than two years.

13. To provide and maintain a navy.

14. To make rules for the government and regulation of the land and naval forces.

15. To provide for calling forth the militia to execute the laws of the Union, suppress insurrections, and repel invasions.

16. To provide for organizing, arming, and disciplining the militia, and for governing such part of them as may be employed in the service of the United States, reserving to the States respectively the appointment of the officers, and the authority of training the militia according to the discipline prescribed by Congress.

17. To exercise exclusive legislation in all cases whatsoever over such district (not exceeding ten miles square) as may, by cession of particular States and the acceptance of Congress, become the seat of Government of the United States, and to exercise like authority over all places purchased by the consent of the Legislature of the State in which the same shall be, for the erection of forts, magazines, arsenals, dry docks, and other needful buildings.

18. To make all laws which shall be necessary and proper for carrying into execution the foregoing powers, and all other powers vested by this Constitution in the Government of the United States, or in any department or officer thereof.

Immigrants, How Admitted.—SECTION IX. **1.** The migration or importation of such persons as any of the States now existing shall think proper to admit, shall not be prohibited by the Congress prior to the year one thousand eight hundred and eight, but a tax or duty may be imposed on such importation, not exceeding ten dollars for each person.

Habeas Corpus.—2. The privilege of the writ of habeas corpus shall not be suspended, unless when in cases of rebellion or invasion the public safety may require it.

Attainder.—3. No bill of attainder or ex post facto law shall be passed.

Direct Taxes.—4. No capitation or other direct tax shall be laid, unless in proportion to the census or enumeration hereinbefore directed to be taken.

Regulations Regarding Customs Duties.—5. No tax or duty shall be laid on articles exported from any State.

6. No preference shall be given by any regulation of commerce or revenue to the ports of one State over those of another, nor shall vessels bound to or from one State be obliged to enter, clear, or pay duties in another.

Moneys, How Drawn.—7. No money shall be drawn from the Treasury but in consequence of appropriations made by law; and a regular statement and account of the receipts and expenditures of all public money shall be published from time to time.

Titles of Nobility Prohibited.—8. No title of nobility shall be granted by the United States. And no person holding any office of profit or trust under them shall, without the consent of the Congress, accept of any present, emolument, office, or title, of any kind whatever, from any king, prince, or foreign state.

Powers of States Defined.—Section X. 1. No State shall enter into any treaty, alliance, or confederation; grant letters of marque and reprisal; coin money; emit bills of credit; make anything but gold and silver coin a tender in payment of debts; pass any bill of attainder, ex post facto law, or law impairing the obligation of contracts, or grant any title of nobility.

2. No State, shall, without the consent of the Congress, lay any impost or duties on imports or exports, except what may be absolutely necessary for executing its inspection laws; and the net produce of all duties and imposts, laid by any State on imports or exports, shall be for the use of the Treasury of the United States; and all such laws shall be subject to the revision and control of the Congress.

3. No State shall, without the consent of Congress, lay any duty of tonnage, keep troops or ships of war in time of peace, enter into any agreement or compact with another State, or with a foreign power, or engage in war, unless actually invaded, or in such imminent danger as will not admit of delay.

ARTICLE II

Executive Power, in Whom Vested.—Section I. 1. The Executive power shall be vested in a President of the United

States of America. He shall hold his office during the term of four years, and, together with the Vice-President, chosen for the same term, be elected as follows:

Electors.—2. Each State shall appoint, in such manner as the Legislature thereof may direct, a number of electors, equal to the whole number of Senators and Representatives to which the State may be entitled in the Congress; but no Senator or Representative or person holding an office of trust or profit under the United States shall be appointed an elector.

Proceedings of Electors.—Proceedings of the House of Representatives.—3. The electors shall meet in their respective States and vote by ballot for two persons, of whom one at least shall not be an inhabitant of the same State with themselves. And they shall make a list of all the persons voted for, and of the number of votes for each, which list they shall sign and certify, and transmit, sealed, to the seat of the Government of the United States, directed to the President of the Senate. The President of the Senate shall, in the presence of the Senate and House of Representatives, open all the certificates, and the votes shall then be counted. The person having the greatest number of votes shall be the President, if such number be a majority of the whole number of electors appointed, and if there be more than one who have such majority, and have an equal number of votes, then the House of Representatives shall immediately choose by ballot one of them for President; and if no person have a majority, then from the five highest on the list the said House shall in like manner choose the President. But in choosing the President, the vote shall be taken by States, the representation from each State having one vote. A quorum, for this purpose shall consist of a member or members from two-thirds of the States, and a majority of all the States shall be necessary to a choice. In every case, after the choice of the President, the person having the greatest number of votes of the electors shall be the Vice-President. But if there should remain two or more who have equal votes, the Senate shall choose from them by ballot the Vice-President.*

Time of Choosing Electors.—4. The Congress may determine

---

* This clause is superseded by Article XII, Amendments.

the time of choosing the electors, and the day on which they shall give their votes, which day shall be the same throughout the United States.

Qualifications of the President.—5. No person except a natural-born citizen, or a citizen of the United States at the time of the adoption of this Constitution, shall be eligible to the office of President; neither shall any person be eligible to that office who shall not have attained to the age of thirty-five years and been fourteen years a resident within the United States.

Provision in Case of His Disability.—6. In case of the removal of the President from office, or of his death, resignation, or inability to discharge the powers and duties of the said office, the same shall devolve on the Vice-President and the Congress may by law provide for the case of removal, death, resignation, or inability, both of the President and Vice-President, declaring what officer shall then act as President, and such officer shall act accordingly, until the disability be removed or a President shall be elected.

Salary of the President.—7. The President shall, at stated times, receive for his services a compensation which shall neither be increased nor diminished during the period for which he shall have been elected, and he shall not receive within that period any other emolument from the United States, or any of them.

Oath of the President.—8. Before he enter on the execution of his office he shall take the following oath or affirmation:

"I do solemnly swear (or affirm) that I will faithfully execute the office of President of the United States, and will, to the best of my ability, preserve, protect, and defend the Constitution of the United States."

Duties of the President.—SECTION II. 1. The President shall be Commander-in-Chief of the Army and Navy of the United States, and of the militia of the several States when called into the actual service of the United States; he may require the opinion, in writing, of the principal officer in each of the executive departments upon any subject relating to the duties of their respective offices, and he shall have power to grant reprieves

NJ

and pardons for offences against the United States except in cases of impeachment.

May Make Treaties, Appoint Ambassadors, Judges, etc.— 2. He shall have power, by and with the advice and consent of the Senate, to make treaties, provided two-thirds of the Senators present concur; and he shall nominate, and by and with the advice and consent of the Senate, shall appoint ambassadors, other public ministers and consuls, judges of the Supreme Court, and all other officers of the United States whose appointments are not herein otherwise provided for, and which shall be established by law; but the Congress may by law vest the appointment of such inferior officers as they think proper in the President alone, in the courts of law, or in the heads of departments.

May Fill Vacancies.—3. The President shall have power to fill up all vacancies that may happen during the recess of the Senate by granting commissions, which shall expire at the end of their next session.

May Make Recommendations to and Convene Congress.— SECTION III. He shall from time to time give to the Congress information of the State of the Union, and recommend to their consideration such measures as he shall judge necessary and expedient; he may, on extraordinary occasions, convene both Houses, or either of them, and in case of disagreement between them, with respect to the time of adjournment, he may adjourn them to such time as he shall think proper; he shall receive ambassadors and other public ministers; he shall take care that the laws be faithfully executed, and shall commission all the officers of the United States.

How Officers May Be Removed.—SECTION IV. The President, Vice-President, and all civil officers of the United States shall be removed from office on impeachment for, and conviction of, treason, bribery, or other high crimes and misdemeanors.

ARTICLE III

Judicial Power, How Vested.—SECTION I. The judicial power of the United States shall be vested in one Supreme Court, and in such inferior courts as the Congress may from time to time ordain and establish. The judges, both of the Supreme and inferior courts, shall hold their offices during good behavior, and shall, at stated times, receive for their services a compensation which shall not be diminished during their continuance in office.

To What Cases it Extends.—SECTION II. 1. The judicial power shall extend to all cases, in law and equity, arising under this Constitution, the laws of the United States, and treaties made, or which shall be made, under their authority; to all cases affecting ambassadors, other public ministers, and consuls; to all cases of admiralty and maritime jurisdiction; to controversies to which the United States shall be a party; to controversies between two or more States; between a State and citizens of another State; between citizens of different States; between citizens of the same State, claiming lands under grants of different States, and between a State, or the citizens thereof, and foreign States, citizens or subjects.

Jurisdiction of the Supreme Court.—2. In all cases affecting ambassadors, other public ministers, and consuls, and those in which a State shall be party, the Supreme Court shall have original jurisdiction. In all the other cases before-mentioned the Supreme Court shall have appellate jurisdiction, both as to law and fact, with such exceptions and under such regulations as the Congress shall make.

Rules Respecting Trials.—3. The trial of all crimes, except in cases of impeachment, shall be by jury, and such trial shall be held in the State where the said crimes shall have been committed; but when not committed within any State the trial shall be at such place or places as the Congress may by law have directed.

Treason Defined.—SECTION III. 1. Treason against the United States shall consist only in levying war against them, or in adhering to their enemies, giving them aid and comfort. No person shall be convicted of treason unless on the testimony of two witnesses to the same overt act, or on confession in open court.

How Punished.—2. The Congress shall have power to declare the punishment of treason, but no attainder of treason shall work

N J

corruption of blood or forfeiture except during the life of the person attainted.

ARTICLE IV

Rights of States and Records.—SECTION I. Full faith and credit shall be given in each State to the public acts, records, and judicial proceedings of every other State. And the Congress may by general laws prescribe the manner in which such acts, records, and proceedings shall be proved, and the effect thereof.

Privileges of Citizens.—SECTION II. 1. The citizens of each State shall be entitled to all privileges and immunities of citizens in the several States.

Executive Requisitions.—2. A person charged in any State with treason, felony, or other crime, who shall flee from justice, and be found in another State, shall, on demand of the Executive authority of the State from which he fled, be delivered up, to be removed to the State having jurisdiction of the crime.

Laws Regulating Service or Labor.—3. No person held to service or labor in one State, under the laws thereof, escaping into another, shall, in consequence of any law or regulation therein, be discharged from such service or labor, but shall be delivered up on claim of the party to whom such service or labor may be due.

New States, How Formed and Admitted.—SECTION III. 1. New States may be admitted by the Congress into this Union, but no new State shall be formed or erected within the jurisdiction of any other State, nor any State be formed by the junction of two or more States, or parts of States, without the consent of the Legislatures of the States concerned, as well as of the Congress.

Power of Congress over Public Lands.—2. The Congress shall have power to dispose of and make all needful rules and regulations respecting the territory or other property belonging to the United States; and nothing in this Constitution shall be so construed as to prejudice any claims of the United States, or of any particular State.

Republican Government Guaranteed.—SECTION IV. The United States shall guarantee to every State in this Union a republican form of government and shall protect each of them against invasion; and, on application of the Legislature, or of the Executive (when the Legislature cannot be convened), against domestic violence.

ARTICLE V

Constitution, How Amended.—The Congress, whenever two-thirds of both Houses shall deem it necessary, shall propose amendments to this Constitution, or, on the application of the Legislatures of two-thirds of the several States, shall call a convention for proposing amendments, which, in either case, shall be valid to all intents and purposes, as part of this Constitution, when ratified by the Legislatures of three-fourths of the several States, or by conventions in three-fourths thereof, as the one or the other mode of ratification may be proposed by the Congress; provided that no amendment which may be made prior to the year one thousand eight hundred and eight shall in any manner affect the first and fourth clauses in the Ninth Section of the First Article; and that no State, without its consent, shall be deprived of its equal suffrage in the Senate.

ARTICLE VI

Validity of Debts Recognized.—1. All debts contracted and engagements entered into before the adoption of this Constitution shall be as valid against the United States under this Constitution as under the Confederation.

Supreme Law of the Land Defined.—2. This Constitution and the laws of the United States which shall be made in pursuance thereof, and all treaties made, or which shall be made, under the authority of the United States, shall be the supreme law of the land, and the judges in every State shall be bound thereby, anything in the Constitution or laws of any State to the contrary notwithstanding.

Oath: of Whom Required and for What.—3. The Senators and Representatives before mentioned, and the members of the several State Legislatures, and all executive and judicial officers, both of the United States, and of the several States, shall be

N J

bound by oath or affirmation to support this Constitution; but no religious test shall ever be required as a qualification to any office or public trust under the United States.

ARTICLE VII

Ratification of the Constitution.—The ratification of the Conventions of nine States shall be sufficient for the establishment of this Constitution between the States so ratifying the same.

DONE in Convention by the unanimous consent of the States present the seventeenth day of September, in the year of our Lord one thousand seven hundred and eighty-seven, and of the Independence of the United States of America the twelfth. In witness whereof we have hereunto subscribed our names

Go: WASHINGTON,
Presidt. and Deputy from Virginia.

AMENDMENTS TO THE CONSTITUTION

Articles in addition to, and Amendment of, the Constitution of the United States of America, proposed by Congress, and ratified by the Legislatures of the several states, pursuant to the Fifth Article of the original Constitution.

ARTICLE I

Religion and Free Speech.—Congress shall make no law respecting an establishment of religion, or prohibiting the free exercise thereof; or abridging the freedom of speech or of the press; or the right of the people peaceably to assemble, and to petition the Government for a redress of grievances.

ARTICLE II

Right to Bear Arms.—A well-regulated militia being necessary to the security of a free State, the right of the people to keep and bear arms shall not be infringed.

ARTICLE III

Soldiers in Time of Peace.—No soldier shall, in time of peace, be quartered in any house without the consent of the owner, nor in time of war but in a manner to be prescribed by law.

ARTICLE IV

Right of Search.—The right of the people to be secure in their persons, houses, papers, and effects, against unreasonable searches and seizures, shall not be violated, and no warrants shall issue but upon probable cause, supported by oath or affirmation, and particularly describing the place to be searched, and the persons or things to be seized.

ARTICLE V

Capital Crimes and Arrest Therefor.—No person shall be held to answer for a capital or other infamous crime, unless on a presentment or indictment of a grand jury, except in cases arising in the land or naval forces, or in the militia when in actual service, in time of war or public danger; nor shall any person be subject for the same offence to be twice put in jeopardy of life or limb; nor shall be compelled in any criminal case to be a witness against himself, nor be deprived of life, liberty, or property, without due process of law; nor shall private property be taken for public use without just compensation.

ARTICLE VI

Right to Speedy Trial.—In all criminal prosecutions, the accused shall enjoy the right to a speedy and public trial, by an impartial jury of the State and district wherein the crime shall have been committed, which district shall have been previously ascertained by law, and to be informed of the nature and cause of the accusation; to be confronted with the witnesses against him; to have compulsory process for obtaining witnesses in his favor, and to have the assistance of council for his defence.

ARTICLE VII

Trial by Jury.—In suits of common law, where the value in controversy shall exceed twenty dollars, the right of trial by jury shall be preserved, and no fact tried by a jury shall be otherwise re-examined in any court of the United States than according to the rules of the common law.

N J

ARTICLE VIII

Excessive Bail.—Excessive bail shall not be required, nor excessive fines imposed, nor cruel and unusual punishments inflicted.

ARTICLE IX

Enumeration of Rights.—The enumeration in the Constitution of certain rights shall not be construed to deny or disparage others retained by the people.

ARTICLE X

Reserved Rights of States.—The powers not delegated to the United States by the Constitution, nor prohibited by it to the States, are reserved to the States respectively, or to the people.

ARTICLE XI

Judicial Power.—The judicial power of the United States shall not be construed to extend to any suit in law or equity, commenced or prosecuted against one of the United States, by citizens of another State, or by citizens or subjects of any foreign State.

ARTICLE XII

Electors in Presidential Elections.—The electors shall meet in their respective States, and vote by ballot for President and Vice-President, one of whom at least shall not be an inhabitant of the same State with themselves; they shall name in their ballots the person voted for as President, and in distinct ballots the person voted for as Vice-President; and they shall make distinct lists of all persons voted for as President, and of all persons voted for as Vice-President, and of the number of votes for each, which lists they shall sign and certify, and transmit, sealed, to the seat of the Government of the United States directed to the President of the Senate; the President of the Senate shall, in the presence of the Senate and House of Representatives, open all the certificates, and the votes shall then be counted; the person having the greatest number of votes for President shall be the President, if such number be a majority of the whole number of electors appointed, and if no person have such majority, then from the persons having the highest numbers, not exceeding three, on the list of those voted for as President, the House of Representatives shall choose immediately, by ballot, the President. But in choosing the President, the votes shall be taken by States, the representation from each State having one vote; a quorum for this purpose shall consist of a member or members from two-thirds of the States, and a majority of all the States shall be necessary to a choice. And if the House of Representatives shall not choose a President, whenever the right of choice shall devolve upon them, before the fourth day of March next following, then the Vice-President shall act as President, as in the case of the death or other constitutional disability of the President. The person having the greatest number of votes as Vice-President shall be the Vice-President, if such number be a majority of the whole number of electors appointed, and if no person have a majority, then from the two highest numbers on the list the Senate shall choose the Vice-President; a quorum for the purpose shall consist of two-thirds of the whole number of Senators, and a majority of the whole number shall be necessary to a choice. But no person constitutionally ineligible to the office of President shall be eligible to that of Vice-President of the United States.

ARTICLE XIII

Slavery Prohibited.—1. Neither slavery nor involuntary servitude, except as a punishment for crime whereof the party shall have been duly convicted, shall exist within the United States, or any place subject to their jurisdiction.

2. Congress shall have power to enforce this article by appropriate legislation.

ARTICLE XIV

Protection for all Citizens.—1. All persons born or naturalized in the United States, and subject to the jurisdiction thereof, are citizens of the United States and of the State wherein they reside. No State shall make or enforce any law which shall abridge the privileges or immunities of citizens of the United

States, nor shall any State deprive any person of life, liberty, or property without due process of law, nor deny to any person within its jurisdiction the equal protection of the laws.

Apportionment of Representatives.—2. Representatives shall be apportioned among the several States according to their respective numbers, counting the whole number of persons in each State, excluding Indians not taxed. But when the right to vote at any election for the choice of electors for President and Vice-President of the United States, Representatives in Congress, the executive and judicial officers of a State, or the members of the Legislature thereof, is denied to any of the male inhabitants of such State, being of twenty-one years of age, and citizens of the United States, or in any way abridged, except for participation in rebellion or other crime, the basis of representation therein shall be reduced in the proportion which the number of such male citizens shall bear to the whole number of male citizens twenty-one years of age in such State.

Rebellion Against the United States.—3. No person shall be a Senator or Representative in Congress, or elector of President and Vice-President, or hold any office, civil or military, under the United States, or under any State, who, having previously taken an oath, as a member of Congress, or as an officer of the United States, or as a member of any State Legislature, or as an executive or judicial officer of any State, to support the Constitution of the United States, shall have engaged in insurrection or rebellion against the same, or given aid and comfort to the enemies thereof. But Congress may, by a vote of two-thirds of each House, remove such disability.

The Public Debt.—4. The validity of the public debt of the United States, authorized by law, including debts incurred for payment of pensions and bounties for services in suppressing insurrection or rebellion shall not be questioned. But neither the United States nor any State shall assume or pay any debt or obligation incurred in aid of insurrection or rebellion against the United States, or any claim for the loss or emancipation of any slave; but all such debts, obligations, and claims shall be held illegal and void.

ARTICLE XV

Right of Suffrage.—1. The right of the citizens of the United States to vote shall not be denied or abridged by the United States or by any State on account of race, color or previous condition of servitude.

2. The Congress shall have power to enforce the provisions of this article by appropriate legislation.

ARTICLE XVI

Income Taxes.—The Congress shall have power to lay and collect taxes on incomes, from whatever source derived, without apportionment among the several States and without regard to any census or enumeration.

ARTICLE XVII

Election of Senators.—The Senate of the United States shall be composed of two Senators from each State, elected by the people thereof, for six years; and each Senator shall have one vote. The electors in each State shall have the qualifications requisite for electors of the most numerous branch of the State Legislatures.

When vacancies happen in the representation of any State in the Senate, the executive authority of such State shall issue writs of election to fill such vacancies, provided that the Legislature of any State may empower the Executive thereof to make temporary appointments until the people fill the vacancies by election as the Legislature may direct.

ARTICLE XVIII

Liquor Prohibition.—1. After one year from the ratification of this article, the manufacture, sale, or transportation of intoxicating liquors within, the importation thereof into, or the exportation thereof from the United States and all territory subject to the jurisdiction thereof for beverage purposes is hereby prohibited.

2. The Congress and the several States shall have concurrent power to enforce this article by appropriate legislation.

3. This article shall be inoperative unless it shall have been ratified as an amendment to the Constitution by the Legislatures

of the several States, as provided in the Constitution, within seven years from the date of the submission hereof to the States by the Congress.

ARTICLE XIX

Woman Suffrage.—1. The right of citizens of the United States to vote shall not be denied or abridged by the United States, or by any State, on account of sex.

Congress shall have power, by appropriate legislation, to enforce the provisions of this article.

ARTICLE XX

Terms of President, Vice-President, Members of Congress, Times of Assembling of Congress.—1. The terms of the President and Vice-President shall end at noon on the 20th day of January, and the terms of Senators and Representatives at noon on the 3d day of January, of the years in which such terms would have ended if this article had not been ratified; and the terms of their successors shall then begin.

2. The Congress shall assemble at least once in every year, and such meeting shall begin at noon on the 3d day of January, unless they shall by law appoint a different day.

3. If, at the time fixed for the beginning of the term of the President, the President elect shall have died, the Vice-President elect shall become President. If a President shall not have been chosen before the time fixed for the beginning of his term, or if the President elect shall have failed to qualify, then the Vice-President elect shall act as President until a President shall have qualified; and the Congress may by law provide for the case wherein neither a President elect nor a Vice-President elect shall have qualified, declaring who shall then act as President, or the manner in which one who is to act shall be selected, and such person shall act accordingly until a President or Vice-President shall have qualified.

4. The Congress may by law provide for the case of the death of any of the persons from whom the House of Representatives may choose a President whenever the right of choice shall have devolved upon them, and for the case of the death

of any of the persons from whom the Senate may choose a Vice-President whenever the right of choice shall have devolved upon them.

ARTICLE XXI

Repeal of Article XVIII.—1. The Eighteenth article of amendment to the Constitution of the United States is hereby repealed.

2. The transportation or importation into any State, territory, or possession of the United States for delivery or use therein of intoxicating liquors, in violation of the laws thereof, is hereby prohibited.

3. This article shall be inoperative unless it shall have been ratified as an amendment to the Constitution by conventions of the several States, as provided in the Constitution within seven years from the date of the submission hereof to the States by the Congress.

RATIFICATION OF THE AMENDMENTS

Articles I to X were declared in force in 1791; Article XI in 1798; Article XII in 1804; Article XIII was proclaimed in December, 1865; Article XIV was proclaimed in July, 1868; Article XV was proclaimed in 1870; Article XVI and Article XVII were proclaimed in 1913; Article XVIII was proclaimed in January, 1919, and took effect in 1920; Article XIX was proclaimed in 1920; Article XX and Article XXI were proclaimed in 1933.

THE INDIAN KING AT HADDONFIELD

Within its walls the Colonial legislature gathered thrice and at the last session substituted the word "state" for the word "colony" in the documents of the new commonwealth.

CONSTITUTION OF THE STATE OF NEW JERSEY

A Constitution agreed upon by the delegates of the people **History** of New Jersey, in convention begun at Trenton on the fourteenth day of May, and continued to the twenty-ninth day of June, in the year of our Lord one thousand eight hundred and forty-four, ratified by the people at an election held on the thirteenth day of August, A.D. 1844, and amended at a special election held on the seventh day of September, A.D. 1875, and at another special election held on the twenty-eighth day of September, A.D. 1897, and at another special election held on the twentieth day of September, A.D. 1927.

The present Constitution of New Jersey was made by a convention which met in Trenton between May 14 and June 29 in 1844. It was ratified by the people at a special election held on August 13, 1884, and amended at other elections held on September 7, 1875, September 28, 1897, and September 20, 1927.

We, the people of the State of New Jersey, grateful to **Preamble** Almighty God for the civil and religious liberty which He hath so long permitted us to enjoy, and looking to Him for a blessing upon our endeavors to secure and transmit the same unimpaired to succeeding generations, do ordain and establish this Constitution:

The preamble of a constitution is an introduction. Notice that this preamble expresses the gratitude which the people feel for their liberties. It also tells you that the people hope that the liberties which they have won may be passed on to coming generations by means of the rules which they set down in the constitution.

N J   (41)

ARTICLE I

RIGHTS AND PRIVILEGES

Natural Rights   1. All men are by nature free and independent, and have certain natural and unalienable rights, among which are those of enjoying and defending life and liberty; acquiring, possessing, and protecting property, and of pursuing and obtaining safety and happiness.

Do you notice how similar this paragraph is to a part of the Declaration of Independence? Democratic government is based on the idea that all people have certain rights and that government should protect them in the enjoyment of those rights. Notice that the rights mentioned here are life, liberty, property, safety, and happiness. Of course a person must not interfere with the rights of others in trying to secure his own rights. He must learn team play.

Political Power   2. All political power is inherent in the people. Government is instituted for the protection, security, and benefit of the people, and they have the right at all times to alter or reform the same, whenever the public good may require it.

In early times many people held that political power belonged to a king or to nobles. Now we claim that the people should rule themselves. They have a right to make the kind of government which they feel will protect and benefit them. Of course, if they can make it, they can change it whenever they think a change is necessary.

Religious Freedom   3. No person shall be deprived of the inestimable privilege of worshipping Almighty God in a manner agreeable to the dictates of his own conscience; nor, under any pretense whatever, to be compelled to attend any place of worship contrary to his faith and judgment; nor shall any person be obliged to pay tithes, taxes, or other rates for building or repairing any church or churches, place or places of worship, or for the maintenance of any minister or ministry, contrary to what he believes to be right, or has deliberately and voluntarily engaged to perform.

4. There shall be no establishment of one religious sect in preference to another; no religious test shall be required as a

qualification for any office or public trust; and no person shall be denied the enjoyment of any civil right merely on account of his religious principles.

These two sections give to every man freedom in his religion. They guarantee also that his religion shall not be considered if he is a candidate for a public office or in connection with any civil right. It would seem very strange to us now for our government to try to force people to go to a certain church. Thomas Jefferson was one of the great believers in religious liberty and he wrote this idea into the constitution of Virginia.

5. Every person may freely speak, write, and publish his **Freedom of Speech** sentiments on all subjects, being responsible for the abuse of that right. No law shall be passed to restrain or abridge the liberty of speech or of the press. In all prosecutions or indictments for libel, the truth may be given in evidence to the jury; and if it shall appear to the jury that the matter charged as libelous is true, and was published with good motives and for justifiable ends, the party shall be acquitted; and the jury shall have the right to determine the law and the fact.

Freedom of speech is another right which people under autocratic governments never had. Every person has a right to criticize what a public official does provided he does not spread lies about the official. If you spread an untruth which another man feels is an injury to him he might sue you in the courts for what is called "libel." If you can prove that what you said is true you would be acquitted; but if it proves to be false you might be fined. Honest discussion makes for good government.

6. The right of the people to be secure in their persons, **Personal Security** houses, papers, and effects, against unreasonable searches and seizures, shall not be violated; and no warrant shall issue but upon probable cause, supported by oath or affirmation, and particularly describing the place to be searched and the papers and things to be seized.

An officer of the law may not enter your house and search for anything unless a warrant is issued. A warrant is a paper

N J

issued by a judge giving the officer the right to make the search. The judge must not issue the warrant unless he is reasonably sure, on someone's oath or affirmation, that you have something illegal in your house. Do you see how this protects you from unjust interference? How would you like to live in a country where a policeman could come in and search your house just because he thinks you have something illegal there?

Right of Trial by Jury

7. The right of a trial by jury shall remain inviolate; but the legislature may authorize the trial of civil suits, when the matter in dispute does not exceed fifty dollars, by a jury of six men.

The right of trial by jury has come to us through many centuries of English law. It means that the twelve men of a jury must all agree before a decision is given. Do you see how this protects you?

Rights of the Accused

8. In all criminal prosecutions the accused shall have the right to a speedy and public trial by an impartial jury; to be informed of the nature and cause of the accusation; to be confronted with the witnesses against him; to have compulsory process for obtaining witnesses in his favor, and to have the assistance of counsel in his defense.

9. No person shall be held to answer for a criminal offense, unless on the presentment or indictment of a grand jury, except in cases of impeachment, or in cases cognizable by justices of the peace, or arising in the army or navy; or in the militia, when in actual service in time of war or public danger.

10. No person shall, after acquittal, be tried for the same offense. All persons shall, before conviction, be bailable by sufficient sureties, except for capital offenses, when the proof is evident or presumption great.

If a man is charged with a crime the constitution gives him certain protection. He is entitled to a fair trial. He must know exactly what he is accused of doing and whatever the witnesses say must be said in the open. He has a right to have a lawyer defend him. If he is poor the judge will provide him with a lawyer. All these rules protect him against an unfair charge.

A "grand jury" is a jury that sits in secret to hear the evidence that the officers of the law bring against accused people. If they think that there is some evidence against a man they so report and then the man is tried before a regular or "trial jury." If they think the evidence is slim, the accused man may be discharged without a trial. In very serious cases such as impeachment of a public officer or in time of war, the grand jury does not act.

Also in minor cases a man may be fined by a justice of the peace. For example, if a man drives his automobile recklessly, the justice of the peace may fine him at once.

Notice that if a man is acquitted he may not be tried again for the same offense. An accused man waiting for trial is allowed to leave the jail if he or his friends are willing to put up money as "bail" to guarantee that he will appear at the trial. Of course this does not apply to serious criminal offenses.

11. The privilege of the writ of habeas corpus shall not be suspended, unless in case of rebellion or invasion the public safety may require it. *Habeas Corpus*

Habeas corpus, a Latin phrase, means "you may have the body." Suppose you are charged with a crime, put in jail, and left there. Your lawyer may apply to a judge to issue an order to have you brought to court to see if there is any good reason to keep you in prison. This protects you from an unjust imprisonment. This privilege cannot be taken away except in time of rebellion or invasion.

12. The military shall be in strict subordination to the civil power. *Freedom from Military Power*

13. No soldier shall, in time of peace, be quartered in any house without the consent of the owner; nor in time of war, except in a manner prescribed by law.

Military government is autocratic, so our forefathers saw that the government set up by the vote of the people must have the final power. Even in time of war things must be done according to law in order that people may not be imposed on.

Treason

14. Treason against the state shall consist only in levying war against it, or in adhering to its enemies, giving them aid and comfort. No person shall be convicted of treason, unless on the testimony of two witnesses to the same overt act, or on confession in open court.

Notice that this definition of treason against the state is the same as that of treason against the United States given in Article III, Section III, of the Constitution of the United States. A man may suggest changes in his government without being a traitor but if he actually makes war on the established government he has committed treason.

Freedom from Excessive Fines and Punishment

15. Excessive bail shall not be required, excessive fines shall not be imposed, and cruel and unusual punishments shall not be inflicted.

Here the citizen is protected against cruelty, unreasonable fines, and heavy bail. If you were arrested for a small offense and the judge fixed the bail at a high amount, do you see how much trouble that would cause you?

Payment for Private Property

16. Private property shall not be taken for public use without just compensation; but land may be taken for public highways as heretofore, until the legislature shall direct compensation to be made.

If the state desires land and cannot agree with the owner on the price the land can be "condemned." This means that commissioners are appointed to value the land and give the owner a fair price. Before 1844 land could be taken for highways without payment. In 1850 the legislature passed a law to give adequate payment for such land.

Imprisonment for Debt

17. No person shall be imprisoned for debt in any action, or on any judgment founded upon contract, unless in cases of fraud; nor shall any person be imprisoned for a militia fine in time of peace.

It was necessary to put this clause into the constitution because in former times many people were thrown into prison for debts, sometimes very small ones. Of course a person can be punished for trying to avoid paying a debt by dishonest methods.

18. The people have a right freely to assemble together, to consult for the common good, to make known their opinions to their representatives, and to petition for redress of grievances. **Right to Assemble and Petition**

This clause is like the one about freedom of speech. It protects people who wish to have peaceful meetings even though they may not agree with the government. If they do not use force people should have the right to discuss matters and to send petitions to their governing officers. This is one of the corner stones of democratic government.

19. No county, city, borough, town, township, or village shall hereafter give any money or property, or loan its money or credit, to or in aid of any individual, association, or corporation, or become security for or be directly or indirectly the owner of any stock or bonds of any association or corporation. **Use of Public Money**

20. No donation of land or appropriation of money shall be made by the state or any municipal corporation to or for the use of any society, association, or corporation whatever.

Public money should be spent for the good of the whole people. It should also be controlled by public officers. These two clauses prevent the state from aiding any private society whether its purpose is business or educational. It is a very good safeguard of the money of the people.

21. This enumeration of rights and privileges shall not be construed to impair or deny others retained by the people. **Saving Clause**

This means that by stating these rights the people do not give up all other rights. Other rights may be recognized as just, even though not written in the constitution. Do you see that the makers of the constitution constantly had in mind protecting the people against oppression?

N J

ARTICLE II

RIGHT OF SUFFRAGE

Suffrage   1. Right of Suffrage.   Every male citizen of the United States, of the age of twenty-one years, who shall have been a resident of this state one year, and of the county in which he claims his vote five months, next before the election, shall be entitled to vote for all officers that now are, or hereafter may be, elective by the people; provided, that no person in the military, naval, or marine service of the United States shall be considered a resident in this state, by being stationed in any garrison, barrack, or military or naval place or station within this state; and no pauper, idiot, insane person, or person convicted of a crime which now excludes him from being a witness unless pardoned or restored by law to the right of suffrage, shall enjoy the right of an elector; and provided further, that in time of war no elector in the actual military service of the state, or of the United States, in the army or navy thereof, shall be deprived of his vote by reason of his absence from such election district; and the legislature shall have power to provide the manner in which, and the time and place at which, such absent electors may vote, and for the return and canvass of their votes in the election districts in which they respectively reside.

In order to vote in New Jersey a person must be—
   (a) a citizen of the United States;
   (b) twenty-one years of age;
   (c) a resident of the state for one year;
   (d) a resident of the county in which he votes for five months.

Do you notice that this section restricts voting to *male* citizens?   Look up the Nineteenth Amendment to the Constitution of the United States.   This amendment gave women the right to vote and must be obeyed by the state even when its own constitution does not provide for woman suffrage. You see, therefore, how the states have given up some of their rights to the federal government.

Bribery   2. The legislature may pass laws to deprive persons of the right of suffrage who shall be convicted of bribery.

Suppose a man pays a legislator to vote for a certain bill or a policeman to set him free when arrested. Such a payment is called a "bribe" and is so serious that a man may lose his vote because of it.

ARTICLE III

DISTRIBUTION OF THE POWERS OF GOVERNMENT

1. The powers of the government shall be divided into three distinct departments—the legislative, executive, and judicial; and no person or persons belonging to, or constituting one of these departments, shall exercise any of the powers properly belonging to either of the others, except as herein expressly provided.

Depart-ments of Govern-ment

Notice how this division of the duties of government into three departments follows the plan of the national government. Thus we have the legislative (law making), executive (law enforcing) and judicial (law interpreting) departments. The departments are not to interfere one with another. If each does its own work there will be no confusion and the government will run smoothly.

ARTICLE IV

LEGISLATIVE

SECTION I

1. The legislative power shall be vested in a senate and general assembly.

The Legis-lature

There are two branches in the legislature just as there are in Congress. Notice that one is called the senate and the other the general assembly.

2. No person shall be a member of the senate who shall not have attained the age of thirty years, and have been a citizen and inhabitant of the state for four years, and of the county for which he shall be chosen one year, next before his election; and no person shall be a member of the general assembly who shall not have attained the age of twenty-one years, and been a citizen and inhabitant of the state for two years, and of the

Qualifica-tions

county for which he shall be chosen for one year next before his election; provided, that no person shall be eligible as a member of either house of the legislature, who shall not be entitled to the right of suffrage.

Members of the legislature must be legal voters. In addition to this they must have the following qualifications:

	SENATE	GENERAL ASSEMBLY
Age.............................	30	21
Citizen and inhabitant of state.....	4 years	2 years
Citizen and inhabitant of county...	1 year	1 year

Elections   3. Members of the senate and general assembly shall be elected yearly and every year, on the first Tuesday after the first Monday in November; and the two houses shall meet separately on the second Tuesday in January next after the said day of election, at which time of meeting the legislative year shall commence; but the time of holding such election may be altered by the legislature.

This clause fixes the annual election day and the date for the beginning of the legislature. Notice that the legislature has the power to change the date of election if it desires to do so.

SECTION II

The Senate   1. The senate shall be composed of one senator from each county in the state, selected by the legal voters of the counties, respectively, for three years.

One senator from each county makes a senate of 21 members. Senators are elected for three years.

How Classified   2. As soon as the senate shall meet after the first election to be held in pursuance of this constitution, they shall be divided as equally as may be into three classes. The seats of the senators of the first class shall be vacated at the expiration of the first year; of the second class at the expiration of the second year; and of the third class at the expiration of the third year, so that one class may be elected every year; and if vacancies happen, by resignation or otherwise, the persons elected to supply such vacancies shall be elected for the unexpired terms only.

This clause was put in so that the seats of one third of the senators would be vacant each year. Thus, you see that during each new session at least two thirds of the members of the senate have had experience.

SECTION III

1. The general assembly shall be composed of members annually elected by the legal voters of the counties, respectively, who shall be apportioned among the said counties as nearly as may be according to the number of their inhabitants. The present apportionment shall continue until the next census of the United States shall have been taken, and an apportionment of members of the general assembly shall be made by the legislature at its first session after the next and every subsequent enumeration or census and when made shall remain unaltered until another enumeration shall have been taken; provided, that each county shall at all times be entitled to one member; and the whole number of members shall never exceed sixty.

The General Assembly

Each county elects members to the general assembly according to its population. This apportionment has to be made over after each decade when the United States census is taken. At present the representation is as follows:

County		County	
Atlantic	2	Mercer	3
Bergen	4	Middlesex	3
Burlington	1	Monmouth	2
Camden	3	Morris	1
Cape May	1	Ocean	1
Cumberland	1	Passaic	5
Essex	12	Salem	1
Gloucester	1	Somerset	1
Hudson	11	Sussex	1
Hunterdon	1	Union	4
		Warren	1
Total			**60**

N J

SECTION IV

Vacancies

1. Each house shall direct writs of election for supplying vacancies, occasioned by death, resignation, or otherwise; but if vacancies occur during the recess of the legislature, the writs may be issued by the governor, under such regulations as may be prescribed by law.

This clause provides for the election of a member of the legislature to fill a vacancy.

Power to Decide Elections Quorum

2. Each house shall be the judge of the elections, returns, and qualifications of its own members, and a majority of each shall constitute a quorum to do business; but a smaller number may adjourn from day to day, and may be authorized to compel the attendance of absent members, in such manner, and under such penalties, as each house may provide.

If an election were disputed each house in the legislature has power to decide who has been legally elected. A majority is one more than half the number of members and this majority must be present to make a quorum and conduct business.

Officers and Rules

3. Each house shall choose its own officers, determine the rules of its proceedings, punish its members for disorderly behavior, and, with the concurrence of two thirds, may expel a member.

Here, each house is given power to organize and discipline itself.

Records

4. Each house shall keep a journal of its proceedings, and from time to time publish the same; and the yeas and nays of the members of either house on any question shall, at the desire of one fifth of those present, be entered on the journal.

Any citizen can find out what goes on in the legislature by reading the official Journal. A member's vote on any question is recorded if one fifth of those present request. Thus his vote is a matter of permanent record.

5. Neither house, during the session of the legislature, shall, without the consent of the other, adjourn for more than three days, nor to any other place than that in which the two houses shall be sitting. **Adjournments**

This clause makes it impossible for one house to adjourn for an indefinite period and thus hold up public business.

6. All bills and joint resolutions shall be read three times in each house, before the final passage thereof; and no bill or joint resolution shall pass unless there be a majority of all the members of each body personally present and agreeing thereto; and the yeas and nays of the members voting on such final passage shall be entered on the journal. **Reading of Bills**

You often hear that a bill has had its first reading, its second reading, or its third reading. This shows you how far along the bill has gone. Notice that in final passage the vote of every member is recorded. A majority of the entire membership must vote favorably on a bill before it can be considered passed. This means eleven votes in the senate and thirty-one in the assembly.

7. Members of the senate and general assembly shall receive annually the sum of five hundred dollars during the time for which they shall have been elected and while they shall hold their office, and no other allowance or emolument, directly or indirectly, for any purpose whatever. The president of the senate and the speaker of the house of assembly shall, in virtue of their offices, receive an additional compensation, equal to one third of their allowance as members. **Salary**

The state does not pay high salaries to the members of the legislature. This is one way by which a citizen can serve his state. Men consider it an honor to be selected for such service.

8. Members of the senate and general assembly shall, in all cases except treason, felony, and breach of the peace, be privileged from arrest during their attendance at the sitting of their respective houses, and in going to and returning from **Privileges of Members**

N J

the same; and for any speech or debate, in either house, they shall not be questioned in any other place.

Except for serious offenses members of the legislature are free from arrest. Likewise they are free to express their opinions in the legislature without fear. Notice how much is said in the constitution to protect the freedom of people to speak and work peacefully for what they think is right.

SECTION V

Appointment to Office

1. No member of the senate or general assembly shall, during the time for which he was elected, be nominated or appointed by the governor or by the legislature in joint meeting, to any civil office under the authority of this state which shall have been created, or the emoluments whereof shall have been increased, during such time.

This is a wise clause because it makes it impossible for members of the legislature to secure positions for themselves or to raise the salary of a position for later advantage to themselves.

Vacation of Seat

2. If any member of the senate or general assembly shall be elected to represent this state in the Senate or House of Representatives of the United States, and shall accept thereof, or shall accept of any office or appointment under the government of the United States, his seat in the legislature of this state shall thereby be vacated.

A person could not give proper attention to work in both the national and state government, so this is a wise clause.

People Not Eligible to the Legislature

3. No justice of the supreme court, nor judge of any other court, sheriff, justice of the peace, nor any person or persons possessed of any office of profit under the government of this state, shall be entitled to a seat either in the senate or in the general assembly; but, on being elected and taking his seat his office shall be considered vacant; and no person holding any office of profit under the government of the United States shall be entitled to a seat in either house.

Here, again we note the intention of keeping people from holding executive or judicial offices or federal positions and at the same time being a member of the legislature. The legislature must be free to regulate the conditions under which the officials of the other departments work.

SECTION VI

1. **Revenue bills originate in house of assembly.** All bills for raising revenue shall originate in the house of assembly; but the senate may propose or concur with amendments, as on other bills.

Revenue Bills

Just as in the national government revenue bills must start in the lower house. Of course, the senate may amend a revenue bill and ask the assembly to approve its amendments.

2. No money shall be drawn from the treasury but for appropriations made by law.

Protection to the State's Money

3. The credit of the state shall not be directly or indirectly loaned in any case.

Paragraph (2) prevents anybody from getting money from the state unless the payment has been authorized by the legislature.

Paragraph (3) prevents the use of the state's credit for any private interest.

4. The legislature shall not, in any manner, create any debt or debts, liability or liabilities, of the state which shall, singly or in the aggregate with any previous debts or liabilities, at any time exceed one hundred thousand dollars, except for purposes of war, or to repel invasion, or to suppress insurrection, unless the same shall be authorized by a law for some single object or work, to be distinctly specified therein; which law shall provide the ways and means, exclusive of loans, to pay the interest of such debt or liability as it falls due, and also to pay and discharge the principal of such debt or liability within thirty-five years from the time of the contracting thereof, and shall be

Creation of Debt

irrepealable until such debt or liability, and the interest thereon, are fully paid and discharged; and no such law shall take effect until it shall, at a general election, have been submitted to the people, and have received the sanction of a majority of all the votes cast for and against it at such election; and all money to be raised by the authority of such law shall be applied only to the specific object stated therein, and to the payment of the debt thereby created. This section shall not be construed to refer to any money that has been, or may be, deposited with this state by the government of the United States.

Do you see how this section makes it necessary for the people to approve the expenditure of large sums of money? Bond issues for roads or bridges, for example must be voted by the people. It is wise also to provide that provisions for paying debts within thirty-five years must be made. Debts should be paid as promptly as possible.

Zoning Ordinance

5. The legislature may enact general laws under which municipalities, other than counties, may adopt zoning ordinances limiting and restricting to specified districts and regulating therein, buildings and structures, according to their construction, and the nature and extent of their use, and the exercise of such authority shall be deemed to be within the police power of the state. Such laws shall be subject to repeal or alteration by the legislature.

This paragraph is an amendment approved by the people in September, 1927. Its purpose is to allow the legislature to make laws so that cities and other municipalities may make zoning districts. These districts are necessary so that an area may be restricted to residences without having factories and other undesirable buildings erected in that area.

SECTION VII

Divorce

1. No divorce shall be granted by the legislature.

This clause keeps the question of divorce in the hands of the courts. If the legislature could grant divorces the members would be subject to a great many bothersome pleas.

2. No lottery shall be authorized by the legislature or Lotteries otherwise, in this state, and no ticket in any lottery shall be bought or sold within this state, nor shall pool-selling, book-making, or gambling of any kind be authorized or allowed within this state, nor shall any gambling device, practice, or game of chance now prohibited by law be legalized, or the remedy, penalty, or punishment now provided therefor be in any way diminished.

This clause recognizes the evils of gambling. People should wish to earn the money which they receive. There is not much satisfaction in trying to get something for nothing.

3. The legislature shall not pass any bill of attainder, Protection of ex *post facto* law, or law impairing the obligation of contracts, the Courts or depriving a party of any remedy for enforcing a contract which existed when the contract was made.

A bill of attainder is a law by a legislature inflicting punishment, without a court trial. An *ex post facto* law is a law which may be used to punish a man for something he did before the law was passed. You can see what confusion we should have if the legislature should interfere with our courts in their administration of law.

4. To avoid improper influences which may result from Protection intermixing in one and the same act such things as have no Against Inaccurate proper relation to each other, every law shall embrace but one Law object, and that shall be expressed in the title. No law shall Making be revived or amended by reference to its title only; but the act revived, or the section or sections amended, shall be inserted at length. No general law shall embrace any provisions of a private, special, or local character. No act shall be passed which shall provide that any existing law, or any part thereof, shall be made or deemed a part of the act, or which shall enact that any existing law, or any part thereof, shall be applicable, except by inserting it in such act.

All of these provisions are for the purpose of having our laws clear and accurate. Without such a clause an unwise statement which would not be noticed might be slipped into a bill. A great many bills are presented at each session of the legislature and care must be taken that each bill contains only one object. In this way business can be done in an accurate way.

Form of a Law

5. The laws of this state shall begin in the following style: "Be it enacted by the senate and general assembly of the State of New Jersey."

This clause provides for a uniform manner of writing the introduction to a bill.

Public Schools

6. The fund for the support of free schools, and all money, stock, and other property which may hereafter be appropriated for that purpose, or received into the treasury under the provision of any law heretofore passed to augment the said fund, shall be securely invested and remain a perpetual fund; and the income thereof, except so much as it may be judged expedient to apply to an increase of the capital, shall be annually appropriated to the support of public free schools, for the equal benefit of all the people of the state; and it shall not be competent for the legislature to borrow, appropriate, or use the said fund, or any part thereof, for any other purpose, under any pretense whatever. The legislature shall provide for the maintenance and support of a thorough and efficient system of free public schools for the instruction of all the children in this state between the ages of five and eighteen years.

This is a very important clause because it makes the state responsible for providing education for all children between five and eighteen years of age. You will notice also that it protects all school money so that it cannot be used for other purposes. In order that people can be good citizens they must be educated.

Protection of Minors

7. No private or special law shall be passed authorizing the sale of any lands belonging in whole or in part to a minor or minors, or other persons who may at the time be under any legal disability to act for themselves.

A person under legal age for doing business is here protected against loss of property.

8. Individuals or private corporations shall not be author- **Protection of Property Owners** ized to take private property for public use, without just compensation first made to the owners.

Even though a company like a railroad serves the public it must make a just payment for any property it takes.

9. No private, special, or local bill shall be passed unless **Special Bills** public notice of the intention to apply therefor, and of the general object thereof, shall have been previously given. The legislature, at the next session after the adoption hereof, and from time to time thereafter, shall prescribe the time and mode of giving such notice, the evidence thereof, and how such evidence shall be preserved.

Here the citizens of the state are protected against those who sometimes wish to secure special legislation for their own benefit. Publicity of such bills often defeats them. Note that citizens must keep their eyes open so that the interest of the whole public will be protected.

10. The legislature may vest in the circuit courts, or courts **Chancery Powers** of common pleas within the several counties of this State, chancery powers, so far as relates to the foreclosure of mortgages and sale of mortgaged premises.

This means that the legislature may give to certain courts powers to see that justice is done even when there are no exact items in the law which cover a certain case.

11. The legislature shall not pass private, local, or special **Laws Not to Be Passed** laws in any of the following enumerated cases; that is to say:
Laying out, opening, altering, and working roads or highways.
Vacating any road, town plot, street, alley, or public grounds.
Regulating the internal affairs of towns and counties; appointing local offices or commissions to regulate municipal affairs.

N 3

Selecting, drawing, summoning, or empaneling grand or petit jurors.

Creating, increasing, or decreasing the percentage or allowance of public officers during the term for which said officers were elected or appointed.

Changing the law of descent.

Granting to any corporation, association, or individual any exclusive privilege, immunity, or franchise whatever.

Granting to any corporation, association, or individual the right to lay down railroad tracks.

Providing for changes of venue in civil or criminal cases.

Providing for the management and support of free public schools.

The legislature shall pass general laws providing for the cases enumerated in this paragraph, and for all other cases which, in its judgment, may be provided for by general laws. The legislature shall pass no special act conferring corporate powers, but they shall pass general laws under which corporations may be organized and corporate powers of every nature obtained, subject, nevertheless, to repeal or alteration at the will of the legislature.

This whole paragraph is for the purpose of preventing legislation which will take care of or benefit single cases. The legislature should pass general laws. Then private companies or individual interests may all be on the same basis. This makes for fairness and equality of opportunity.

Assessment of Property

12. Property shall be assessed for taxes under general laws, and by uniform rules, according to its true value.

Property is to be assessed at its true value, that is, what it is worth in the market. This causes a fair distribution of taxes.

SECTION VIII

Oaths of Office

1. Members of the legislature shall, before they enter on the duties of their respective offices, take and subscribe the following oath or affirmation:

"I do solemnly swear (or affirm, as the case may be) that I will support the Constitution of the United States and the constitution of the State of New Jersey, and that I will faithfully discharge the duties of senator (or member of the general assembly, as the case may be) according to the best of my ability."

And members-elect of the senate or general assembly are hereby empowered to administer to each other the said oath or affirmation.

2. Every officer of the legislature shall, before he enters upon his duties, take and subscribe the following oath or affirmation: "I do solemnly promise and swear (or affirm) that I will faithfully, impartially, and justly perform all the duties of the office of ......, to the best of my ability and understanding; that I will carefully preserve all records, papers, writings, or property intrusted to me for safe-keeping by virtue of my office, and make such disposition of the same as may be required by law." **Oath of Officers**

Do you notice that in addition to agreeing to be a faithful supporter of his state a member agrees to support the Constitution of the United States? Thus, we all have a double allegiance.

ARTICLE V

EXECUTIVE

1. The executive power shall be vested in a governor. **Governor**

The governor is the head of the executive branch of the government.

2. The governor shall be elected by the legal voters of this state. The person having the highest number of votes shall be the governor; but if two or more shall be equal and highest in votes, one of them shall be chosen governor by the vote of a majority of the members of both houses in joint meeting. Contested elections for the office of governor shall be determined in such manner as the legislature shall direct by law. When a **Election and Term of Governor**

governor is to be elected by the people, such election shall be held at the time when and at the places where the people shall respectively vote for members of the legislature.

3. The governor shall hold his office for three years, to commence on the third Tuesday of January next ensuing the election for governor by the people, and to end on the Monday preceding the third Tuesday of January, three years thereafter; and he shall be incapable of holding that office for three years next after his term of service shall have expired; and no appointment or nomination to office shall be made by the governor during the last week of his said term.

The governor is elected for a term of three years. It is interesting that a governor may not be a candidate for a second term until three years after his first term of service. In some states this provision does not exist but it was probably put in to prevent a governor from working for his own re-election.

Qualifications

4. The governor shall be not less than thirty years of age, and shall have been for twenty years, at least, a citizen of the United States, and a resident of this state seven years next before his election, unless he shall have been absent during that time on the public business of the United States or of this state.

Notice that the governor must have been a resident of the state much longer than a member of the senate or the assembly.

Salary of the Governor

5. The governor shall, at stated times, receive for his services a compensation which shall be neither increased nor diminished during the period for which he shall have been elected.

A governor should not be able to have his salary raised while in office nor should it be decreased. At present, the governor of New Jersey is paid an annual salary of $10,000.

Powers of the Governor

6. He shall be the commander-in-chief of all the military and naval forces of the state; he shall have power to convene the legislature, or the senate alone, whenever in his opinion public necessity requires it; he shall communicate by message

to the legislature at the opening of each session, and at such
other times as he may deem necessary the condition of the
state, and recommend such measures as he may deem expedient;
he shall take care that the laws be faithfully executed, and
grant, under the great seal of the state, commissions to all
such officers as shall be required to be commissioned.

Besides seeing that laws are enforced the governor has the
duty of recommending legislation and appropriations to the
legislature. Notice that he is the military commander-in-chief
of the state just as the President is of the nation.

7. Every bill which shall have passed both houses shall be
presented to the governor; if he approve he shall sign it, but
if not, he shall return it, with his objections, to the house in
which it shall have originated, who shall enter the objections at
large on their journal, and proceed to reconsider it; if, after such
reconsideration, a majority of the whole number of that house
shall agree to pass the bill, it shall be sent, together with the
objections, to the other house, by which it shall likewise be
reconsidered, and if approved of by a majority of the whole
number of that house, it shall become a law; but in neither
house shall the vote be taken on the same day on which the bill
shall be returned to it; and in all such cases, the votes of both
houses shall be determined by yeas and nays, and the names
of the persons voting for and against the bill shall be entered on
the journal of each house respectively. If any bill shall not be
returned by the governor, within five days (Sunday excepted)
after it shall have been presented to him, the same shall be a
law in like manner as if he had signed it, unless the legislature
by their adjournment prevent its return, in which case it shall
not be a law. If any bill presented to the governor contain
several items of appropriations of money, he may object to one
or more of such items while approving of the other portions of
the bill. In such case he shall append to the bill, at the time
of signing it, a statement of the items to which he objects, and
the appropriation so objected to shall not take effect. If the
legislature be in session he shall transmit to the house in which

Approval of Bills

the bill originated a copy of such statement, and the items objected to shall be separately reconsidered. If, on reconsideration, one or more of such items be approved by a majority of the members elected to each house, the same shall be a part of the law, notwithstanding the objections of the governor. All the provisions of this section in relation to bills not approved by the governor shall apply to cases in which he shall withhold his approval from any item or items contained in a bill appropriating money.

If a governor does not wish to sign a bill he sends it back to the legislature. This is called vetoing a bill. Notice that if a *majority* of both houses repass a bill it becomes a law. In the United States Congress a vetoed bill must receive a two-thirds vote to become a law. Notice also that if the governor keeps a bill five days it becomes a law without his signature. Sometimes several hundred bills are presented to the governor during the closing days of the session of the legislature. He must work fast to consider all of these within the five days allowed.

Ineligibility   8. No member of Congress, or person holding an office under the United States, or this state, shall exercise the office of governor; and in case the governor, or person administering the government shall accept any office under the United States, or this state, his office of governor shall thereupon be vacant. Nor shall he be elected by the legislature to any office under the government of this State or of the United States, during the term for which he shall have been elected governor.

The governor must not hold other state or national offices. He needs to give his undivided attention to his important work.

Power Over Fines, etc.   9. The governor, or person administering the government, shall have power to suspend the collection of fines and forfeitures, and to grant reprieves, to extend until the expiration of a time not exceeding ninety days after conviction; but this power shall not extend to cases of impeachment.

This clause might prevent unjust fines or punishments. The governor could cause delay and thus secure more consideration of a case.

10. The governor, or person administering the government, **Pardons** the chancellor, and the six judges of the court of errors and appeals, or a major part of them, of whom the governor, or person administering the government, shall be one, may remit fines and forfeitures, and grant pardons, after convictions, in all cases except impeachment.

You notice that the governor alone cannot grant a pardon. There must be a majority vote of the group which is named here.

11. The governor and all other civil officers under this **Impeach-** state shall be liable to impeachment for misdemeanor in office **ment** during their continuance in office, and for two years thereafter.

An impeachment is a trial. The trial of a public officer does not occur often, yet it is wise to have all our officers subject to law.

12. In case of the death, resignation, or removal from office **Vacancies in** of the governor, the powers, duties, and emoluments of the office **the Office of** shall devolve upon the president of the senate, and in case of his **Governor** death, resignation, or removal, then upon the speaker of the house of assembly, for the time being, until another governor shall be elected and qualified; but in such case another governor shall be chosen at the next election for members of the legislature, unless such death, resignation, or removal shall occur within thirty days immediately preceding such next election, in which case a governor shall be chosen at the second succeeding election for members of the legislature. When a vacancy happens, during the recess of the legislature, in any office which is to be filled by the governor and senate, or by the legislature, in joint meeting, the governor shall fill such vacancy and the commission shall expire at the end of the next session of the legislature, unless a successor shall be sooner appointed; when a vacancy happens in the office of clerk or surrogate of any county, the governor shall fill such vacancy, and the commission shall expire when a successor is elected and qualified. No person who shall have been nominated to the senate by the governor for any office of trust or profit under the government of this state, and shall not have been confirmed before the recess of the legislature, shall be eligible for appointment to such office during the continuance of such recess.

13. In case of the impeachment of the governor, his absence from the state or inability to discharge the duties of his office, the powers, duties, and emoluments of the office shall devolve upon the president of the senate; and in case of his death, resignation, or removal, then upon the speaker of the house of assembly for the time being, until the governor, absent or impeached, shall return or be acquitted, or until the disqualification or inability shall cease, or until a new governor be elected and qualified.

14. In case of a vacancy in the office of governor from any other cause than those herein enumerated, or in case of the death of the governor-elect before he is qualified into office, the powers, duties, and emoluments of the office shall devolve upon the president of the senate or speaker of the house of assembly, as above provided for, until a new governor be elected and qualified.

These clauses provide for the filling of the office of governor in case of death, resignation, impeachment, or any other cause. You should note that when the legislature is not in session the governor may fill vacancies and thus keep the business of the state going on. But, if the senate does not confirm the nomination before it adjourns the governor may not appoint the same person again. Thus you see that the senate has considerable control over the appointments of the governor.

ARTICLE VI

JUDICIARY

SECTION I

Courts Established 1. The judicial power shall be vested in a court of errors and appeals in the last resort in all causes as heretofore; a court for the trial of impeachments; a court of chancery; a prerogative court; a supreme court; circuit courts, and such inferior courts as now exist, and as may be hereafter ordained and established by law; which inferior courts the legislature may alter or abolish, as the public good shall require.

Here are listed the different courts set up in the state. The court of errors and appeals is the highest or final court.

SECTION II

1. The court of errors and appeals shall consist of the chancellor, the justices of the supreme court, and six judges, or a major part of them; which judges are to be appointed for six years.

Court of Errors and Appeals

2. Immediately after the court shall first assemble, the six judges shall arrange themselves in such manner that the seat of one of them shall be vacated every year, in order that thereafter one judge may be annually appointed.

3. Such of the six judges as shall attend the court shall receive, respectively, a per diem compensation, to be provided by law.

4. The secretary of state shall be the clerk of this court.

5. When an appeal from an order or decree shall be heard, the chancellor shall inform the court, in writing, of the reasons for his order or decree; but he shall not sit as a member, or have a voice in the hearing or final sentence.

6. When a writ of error shall be brought, no justice who has given a judicial opinion in the cause in favor of or against any error complained of, shall sit as a member, or have a voice on the hearing, or for its affirmance or reversal; but the reasons for such opinion shall be assigned to the court in writing.

These clauses, you will note, regulate the composition, compensation, and duties of the court of errors and appeals. When appeals come to this court from lower courts no judge who has passed a judicial opinion on the case in a lower court shall have a vote. Thus a fair hearing is obtained before men who are not influenced one way or the other. Our courts must always decide questions according to their understanding of the law.

SECTION III

Impeachment

1. The house of assembly shall have the sole power of impeaching, by a vote of a majority of all the members; and all impeachments shall be tried by the senate; the members, when sitting for that purpose, to be on oath or affirmation "truly and impartially to try and determine the charge in question according to evidence"; and no person shall be convicted without the concurrence of two thirds of all the members of the senate.

2. Any judicial officer impeached shall be suspended from exercising his office until his acquittal.

3. Judgment in cases of impeachment shall not extend farther than to removal from office, and to disqualification to hold and enjoy any office of honor, profit, or trust under this state; but the party convicted shall, nevertheless, be liable to indictment, trial, and punishment according to law.

4. The secretary of state shall be the clerk of this court.

Do you see that in a case of impeachment the assembly votes first to have the case tried? Then the senate sits as a "court" to try the case. Anyone found guilty of misconduct in office may be removed from office but may not be fined or imprisoned unless the case is carried to an ordinary court of law.

SECTION IV

Court of Chancery

1. The court of chancery shall consist of a chancellor.

The court of chancery is very interesting because it is formed for the purpose of providing justice when the remedies prescribed by courts are not adequate. Notice that the chancellor is the court. He is really the highest legal officer in the state.

2. The chancellor shall be the ordinary or surrogate general, and judge of the prerogative court.

This means that the chancellor is judge of the highest probate court in the state. By probate court is meant a court dealing with wills and the settlement of estates.

3. All persons aggrieved by any order, sentence, or decree of the orphans' court, may appeal from the same, or from any part thereof to the prerogative court; but such order, sentence, or decree shall not be removed into the supreme court, or circuit court if the subject matter thereof be within the jurisdiction of the orphans' court.

Perhaps you can tell by the name "orphans' court" that this court takes care of the property left when a person dies. This paragraph provides for an appeal to the chancellor's court so that a person may secure justice if he thinks he has been wronged in the lower court.

4. The secretary of state shall be the register of the prerogative court, and shall perform the duties required of him by law in that respect.

As in the other courts. the secretary of state is the clerk of this court.

SECTION V

1. The supreme court shall consist of a chief justice and four associate justices. The number of associate justices may be increased or decreased by law, but shall never be less than two.

2. The circuit courts shall be held in every county of this state, by one or more of the justices of the supreme court, or a judge appointed for that purpose. and shall, in all cases within the county except in those of a criminal nature, have common law jurisdiction, concurrent with the supreme court; and any final judgment of a circuit court may be docketed in the supreme

court, and shall operate as a judgment obtained in the supreme court from the time of such docketing.

3. Final judgments in any circuit court may be brought by writ of error into the supreme court, or directly into the court of errors and appeals.

There are now eight associate justices so that the supreme court consists of nine justices.

The supreme court takes care of questions involving all real, personal, or mixed actions at common law. It also has the power to decide whether laws of the legislature have been properly passed or are in accordance with the constitution. The only appeal from this court is to the court of errors and appeals.

The circuit courts have equal authority with the supreme court except in criminal cases. There are now twelve circuit court judges who hold court in different parts of the state.

SECTION VI

Court of Common Pleas 1. There shall be no more than five judges of the inferior court of common pleas in each of the counties in this state, after the terms of the judges of said court now in office shall terminate. One judge for each county shall be appointed every year, and no more, except to fill vacancies, which shall be for the unexpired term only.

2. The commissions for the first appointments of judges of said court shall bear date and take effect on the first day of April next; and all subsequent commissions for judges of said court shall bear date and take effect on the first day of April in every successive year, except commissions to fill vacancies, which shall bear date and take effect when issued.

The court of common pleas holds sessions in each county. This is a busy court because it considers personal disputes and cases relating to bankruptcy, accidents, etc.

Each county has one judge of common pleas.

SECTION VII

1. There may be elected under this consitution two, and not more than five, justices of the peace in each of the townships of the several counties of this state, and in each of the wards, in cities that may vote in wards. When a township or ward contains two thousand inhabitants or less, it may have two justices; when it contains more than two thousand inhabitants, and not more than four thousand, it may have four justices; and when it contains more than four thousand inhabitants, it may have five justices; provided, that whenever any township not voting in wards contains more than seven thousand inhabitants, such township may have an additional justice for each additional three thousand inhabitants above four thousand. *Justices of the Peace*

2. The population of the townships in the several counties of the state and of the several wards shall be ascertained by the last preceding census of the United States, until the legislature shall provide, by law, some other mode of ascertaining it.

Justices of the peace have charge of minor offenses. If a a man is caught violating the Motor Vehicle Act he would probably be taken before a justice of the peace who might fine him. Notice that justices of the peace are elected by the people.

ARTICLE VII

APPOINTING POWER AND TENURE OF OFFICE

SECTION I

MILITIA OFFICERS

1. The legislature shall provide by law for enrolling, organizing, and arming the militia. *Militia Officers and Organization*

2. Captains, subalterns, and non-commissioned officers shall be elected by the members of their respective companies.

3. Field officers of regiments, independent battalions, and squadrons shall be elected by the commissioned officers of their respective regiments, battalions, or squadrons.

N J

4. Brigadier-generals shall be elected by the field officers of their respective brigades.

5. Major-generals, the adjutant-general, and quartermaster-general shall be nominated by the governor, and appointed by him, with the advice and consent of the senate.

6. The legislature shall provide, by law, the time and manner of electing militia officers, and of certifying their elections to the governor, who shall grant their commissions, and determine their rank, when not determined by law; and no commissioned officer shall be removed from office but by the sentence of a court-martial, pursuant to law.

7. In case the electors of subalterns, captains, or field officers shall refuse or neglect to make such elections, the governor shall have power to appoint such officers, and to fill all vacancies caused by such refusal or neglect.

8. Brigade inspectors shall be chosen by the field officers of their respective brigades.

9. The governor shall appoint all militia officers whose appointment is not otherwise provided for in this constitution.

10. Major-generals, brigadier-generals, and commanding officers of regiments, independent battalions, and squadrons shall appoint the staff officers of their divisions, brigades, regiments, independent battalions, and squadrons, respectively.

You know that the United States has an army. The state also has a force called the "militia." In the paragraphs you see the way this force is organized. Notice that officers are elected by various units except that the high officers are appointed by the governor.

SECTION II

CIVIL OFFICERS

Justices, Chancellor, and Judges

1. Justices of the supreme court, chancellor, judges of the court of errors and appeals and judges of the inferior court

of common pleas shall be nominated by the governor, and appointed by him, with the advice and consent of the senate.

The justices of the supreme court and the chancellor shall hold their offices for the term of seven years, shall, at stated times, receive for their services a compensation which shall not be diminished during the term of their appointments; and they shall hold no other office under the government of this state or of the United States.

By having these officers appointed by the governor they are removed from the necessity of making campaigns and appealing for votes. The governor's opinion must be approved by the senate.

2. Judges of the courts of common pleas shall be appointed by the senate and general assembly in joint meeting.[1] **Judges of Common Pleas**

These officers are elected by the legislature in joint session and hold office for three years.

This provision that these judges be appointed by the legislature is disregarded because of an amendment made in 1875 to Paragraph 1 above which provided that these judges be appointed by the governor.

3. The state treasurer and comptroller shall be appointed by the senate and general assembly, in joint meeting. **Treasurer, Comptroller**
They shall hold their offices for three years, and until their successors shall be qualified into office.

---

[1]This provision that the judges of the court of common pleas shall be appointed by the senate and general assembly in joint meeting, which was in the Constitution as ratified in 1844, and never since formally expunged, is disregarded because of the amendment made in 1875 in paragraph one of this section, which provides, *inter alia*, that judges of inferior courts of common pleas shall be nominated by the governor, and appointed by him, with the advice and consent of the senate.
They shall hold their offices for five years; but when appointed to fill vacancies, they shall hold for the unexpired term only.

N J

Attorney General and Others

4. The attorney-general, prosecutors of the pleas, clerk of the supreme court, clerk of the court of chancery, secretary of state and the keeper of the state prison shall be nominated by the governor, and appointed by him, with the advice and consent of the senate.

They shall hold their offices for five years.

The attorney-general represents the state in legal matters. The keeper of the state prison has a great responsibility in providing for the care and discipline of the prisoners.

Reporters

5. The law reporter shall be appointed by the justices of the supreme court, or a majority of them; and the chancery reporter shall be appointed by the chancellor.

They shall hold their offices for five years.

These officers are appointed by the people with whom they work.

Clerks and Surrogates

6. Clerks and surrogates of counties shall be elected by the people of their respective counties, at the annual elections for members of the general assembly.

They shall hold their offices for five years.

Notice that these county officers are elected by the people of the county. The county clerk has a number of duties connected with keeping the records of the business of the county. The surrogate deals with probating wills and the settlement of estates.

Sheriffs and Coroners

7. Sheriffs and coroners shall be elected by the people of their respective counties, at the elections for members of the general assembly, and they shall hold their offices for three years, after which three years must elapse before they can be again capable of serving. Sheriffs shall annually renew their bonds.

These officers are elected by the people. The sheriff is responsible for keeping peace in the county. He should investigate cases of law breaking and arrest the offenders. The coroner has the duty of investigating cases of death under suspicious circumstances.

8. Justices of the peace shall be elected by ballot at the annual meetings of the townships in the several counties of the state, and of the wards in cities that may vote in wards, in such manner and under such regulations as may be hereafter provided by law.

They shall be commissioned for the county, and their commissions shall bear date and take effect on the first day of May next after their election.

They shall hold their offices for five years; but when elected to fill vacancies, they shall hold for the unexpired term only; provided, that the commission of any justice of the peace shall become vacant upon his ceasing to reside in the township in which he was elected.

The first election for justices of the peace shall take place at the next annual town meetings of the townships in the several counties of the state, and of the wards in cities that may vote in wards.

You already know that these officers take care of minor cases.

9. All other officers, whose appointments are not otherwise provided for by law, shall be nominated by the governor, and appointed by him, with the advice and consent of the senate; and shall hold their offices for the time prescribed by law.

When need arises for other officers the governor may appoint.

10. All civil officers elected or appointed pursuant to the provisions of this constitution, shall be commissioned by the governor.

After a person is appointed to an office he receives a paper or "commission" signed by the governor. This shows that he is legally entitled to the office he holds.

11. The term of office of all officers elected or appointed, pursuant to the provisions of this constitution, except when herein otherwise directed, shall commence on the day of the

date of their respective commissions; but no commission for any office shall bear date prior to the expiration of the term of the incumbent of said office.

No person can hold office until his commission has been signed and in force.

ARTICLE VIII
GENERAL PROVISIONS

Secretary of State

1. The secretary of state shall be ex-officio an auditor of the accounts of the treasurer, and as such, it shall be his duty to assist the legislature in the annual examination and settlement of said accounts, until otherwise provided by law.

Here, the secretary of state is given the duty of looking over the accounts of the treasurer to see if they are correct.

Seal of the State

2. The seal of the state shall be kept by the governor or person administering the government, and used by him officially, and shall be called the great seal of the State of New Jersey.

3. All grants and commissions shall be in the name and by the authority of the State of New Jersey, sealed with the great seal, signed by the governor, or person administering the government, and countersigned by the secretary of state, and it shall run thus: "The State of New Jersey to ——————, greeting." All writs shall be in the name of the state; and all indictments shall conclude in the following manner, viz.: "against the peace of this state, the government and dignity of the same."

The seal of the state must be stamped on certain documents before they are valid. Notice that the governor is responsible for keeping this seal.

Date of Operation of Constitution

4. This constitution shall take effect and go into operation on the second day of September, in the year of our Lord one thousand eight hundred and forty-four.

This provision was necessary in order to abolish the old constitution on a given date.

ARTICLE IX

AMENDMENTS

Any specific amendment or amendments to the constitution may be proposed in the senate or general assembly, and if the same shall be agreed to by a majority of the members elected to each of the two houses, such proposed amendment or amendments shall be entered on their journals, with the yeas and nays taken thereon, and referred to the legislature then next to be chosen, and shall be published for three months previous to making such choice, in at least one newspaper of each county, if any be published therein; and if in the legislature next chosen as aforesaid, such proposed amendment or amendments, or any of them, shall be agreed to by a majority of all the members elected to each house, then it shall be the duty of the legislature to submit such proposed amendment or amendments, or such of them as may have been agreed to as aforesaid by the two legislatures, to the people, in such manner and at such time, at least four months after the adjournment of the legislature, as the legislature shall prescribe; and if the people at a special election to be held for that purpose only, shall approve and ratify such amendment or amendments, or any of them, by a majority of the electors qualified to vote for members of the legislature voting thereon, such amendment or amendments so approved and ratified shall become part of the constitution; provided, that if more than one amendment be submitted, they shall be submitted in such manner and form that the people may vote for or against each amendment separately and distinctly; but no amendment or amendments shall be submitted to the people by the legislature oftener than once in five years.

How the Constitution May Be Amended

The makers of the constitution realized that changes of life and of ideas might make it necessary to amend the constitution. On the other hand they thought that amendments should be well thought out and not too easy to make. Notice the number of steps that must be taken before an amendment can be passed. It must be passed by both houses of the legislature not only in one session but in two sessions. It must have publicity. Even after that it must be passed by a majority of the voters at a special election. All amendments must be kept separate so that there will be no confusion. Then if an amendment fails, five years must pass before it is presented again. Thus, an amendment must be very worthy to travel through all of these steps. Notice that the constitution has been amended only three times since 1844.

ARTICLE X

SCHEDULE

Schedule for the Change of Government from the Old Constitution of 1776 to the New One of 1844

That no inconvenience may arise from the change in the constitution of this state, and in order to carry the same into complete operation, it is hereby declared and ordained, that—

1. The common law and statute laws now in force, not repugnant to this constitution, shall remain in force until they expire by their own limitation, or be altered or repealed by the legislature; and all writs, actions, causes of action, prosecutions, contracts, claims and rights of individuals and of bodies corporate, and of the state, and all charters of incorporation, shall continue, and all indictments which shall have been found, or which may hereafter be found, for any crime or offense committed before the adoption of this constitution, may be proceeded upon as if no change had taken place. The several courts of law and equity, except as herein otherwise provided, shall continue with the like powers and jurisdiction as if this constitution had not been adopted.

2. All officers now filling any office or appointment shall continue in the exercise of the duties thereof, according to their respective commissions or appointments, unless by this constitution it is otherwise directed.

3. The present governor, chancellor, and ordinary or surrogate-general and treasurer shall continue in office until successors elected or appointed under this constitution shall be sworn or affirmed into office.

4. In case of the death, resignation, or disability of the present governor, the person who may be vice-president of council at the time of the adoption of this constitution shall continue in office and administer the government until a governor shall have been elected and sworn or affirmed into office under this constitution.

5. The present governor, or in case of his death or inability to act, the vice-president of council, together with the present members of the legislative council and secretary of state, shall constitute a board of state canvassers, in the manner now pro-

vided by law, for the purpose of ascertaining and declaring the result of the next ensuing election for governor, members of the house of representatives, and electors of president and vice-president.

6. The returns of the votes for governor, at the said next ensuing election, shall be transmitted to the secretary of state, the votes counted, and the election declared in the manner now provided by law in the case of the election of electors of president and vice-president.

7. The election of clerks and surrogates, in those counties where the term of office of the present incumbent shall expire previous to the general election of eighteen hundred and forty-five, shall be held at the general election next ensuing the adoption of this constitution; the result of which election shall be ascertained in the manner now provided by law for the election of sheriffs.

8. The elections for the year eighteen hundred and forty-four shall take place as now provided by law.

9. It shall be the duty of the governor to fill all vacancies in office happening between the adoption of this constitution and the first session of the senate, and not otherwise provided for, and the commissions shall expire at the end of the first session of the senate, or when successors shall be elected or appointed and qualified.

10. The restriction of the pay of members of the legislature, after forty days from the commencement of the session, shall not be applied to the first legislature convened under this constitution.

11. Clerks of counties shall be clerks of the inferior courts of common pleas and quarter sessions of the several counties, and perform the duties, and be subject to the regulations now required of them by law until otherwise ordained by the legislature.

12. The legislature shall pass all laws necessary to carry into effect the provisions of this constitution.

All these paragraphs were for the purpose of changing from the old constitution to the new one. It was necessary that the government go on until all of the provisions of the new constitution could be put in force. Notice the importance of Paragraph 12 in giving the legislature the right to pass all laws necessary to carry out the provisions of the constitution.

State of New Jersey:

I, Joseph F. S. Fitzpatrick, Secretary of State of the State of New Jersey, do hereby certify the foregoing to be a true copy of the Constitution of the State of New Jersey as amended, as the same is taken from and compared with the original Constitution and amendments thereto, now remaining on file in my office.

[L. S.]   In testimony whereof, I have hereunto set my hand and affixed my official seal, this first day of August A.D. nineteen hundred and twenty-six.

JOSEPH F. S. FITZPATRICK.

HISTORY OF THE FLAG OF THE UNITED STATES

The Flag of the United States of America is the third oldest of the national standards of the world; older than the Union Jack of Great Britain or the Tricolor of France.

During the early days of the Revolutionary War a variety of flags were used by the different colonies and military commands. Prominent among these were the "Pine Tree" and "Rattlesnake" flags with various arrangements and mottoes.

Late in 1775 a committee of Congress with Benjamin Franklin at the head, after consulting with Washington in command of the army at Cambridge, decided upon the form for a new flag. This flag consisted of thirteen stripes, red and white, with the crosses of St. George and St. Andrew on a blue field in the canton or union. This preceded the Declaration of Independence and indicated that the colonies had not wholly broken from the mother country. This flag was first unfurled by Washington, January 2, 1776. It was probably this flag which was raised by Paul Jones on his vessel and carried by the American fleet which sailed out of Philadelphia in February, 1776.

During 1776 and 1777 a number of flags with thirteen stripes came into use and the need of a definite national emblem was realized. On June 14, 1777, Congress passed an act stating "That the flag of the thirteen United States be thirteen stripes, alternate red and white, that the union be thirteen stars, white in a blue field, representing a new constellation." This was the birthday of the Flag as we now know it and June 14 is now celebrated as "Flag Day." This new flag was first displayed on land at Fort Stanwix, New York, and it remained the national standard until 1795.

In the meantime Vermont and Kentucky had become states, and on January 13, 1794, Congress voted that the flag should have fifteen stripes and fifteen stars. This flag remained in use for twenty-three years, and it was "The Star-Spangled Banner" of which Francis Scott Key wrote in 1814.

In April, 1818, Congress passed an act providing that the flag should have the thirteen horizontal stripes, alternate red and white, and that the union should display twenty stars, representing the number of states then in the Union. It also provided that on the admission of every new state to the Union a star should be added on the following July 4th and this has been the regulation ever since, accounting now for the forty-eight stars shown.

PLEDGE OF ALLEGIANCE TO THE FLAG

I pledge allegiance to the Flag of the United States of America, and to the Republic for which it stands, one Nation, indivisible, with liberty and justice for all.

THE CODE OF THE FLAG OF THE UNITED STATES

The following flag code was drawn up and endorsed in 1923 by the Flag Conference, composed of representatives of the American Legion and other patriotic bodies. In 1924, this code was revised and confirmed by a second conference, and subsequently approved by United States Army and Navy experts. It is generally accepted and used in schools and by patriotic bodies throughout the country.

PROPER MANNER OF DISPLAYING THE FLAG

1. The Flag should be displayed only from sunrise to sunset, or between such hours as may be designated by proper authority. It should be hoisted briskly but should be lowered ceremoniously. The Flag should be displayed on all National and State holidays and on historic and special occasions. (However, being the emblem of our country, it ought to fly from every flagpole every day throughout the year, weather permitting).

2. When carried in a procession with another flag or flags, the Flag of the United States of America should be either on the marching right, i. e., the Flag's own right, or when there is a line of other flags, the Flag of the United States of America may be in front of the center of that line.

3. When displayed with another flag against a wall from crossed staffs, the Flag of the United States of America should be on the right, the Flag's own right, and its staff should be in front of the staff of the other flag.

4. When a number of flags of States or cities or pennants are grouped and displayed from staffs with the Flag of the United States of America, the latter should be at the center or at the highest point of the group.

5. When flags of States or cities or pennants of societies are flown on the same halyard with the Flag of the United States of America, the latter should always be at the peak.

When flown from adjacent staffs the Flag of the United States of America should be hoisted first and lowered last. No such flag or pennant flown in the former position should be placed above, or in the latter position to the right of the Flag of the United States of America, i. e., to the observer's left.

6. **When flags of two or more nations are displayed** they should be flown from separate staffs of the same height and the flags should be of approximately equal size. International usage forbids the display of the flag of one nation above that of another nation in time of peace.

7. **When the Flag is displayed from a staff projecting horizontally or at an angle** from the window sill, balcony, or front of building, the union of the Flag should go clear to the peak of the staff unless the Flag is at half-staff. (When the Flag is suspended over a sidewalk from a rope, extending from a house to a pole at the edge of the sidewalk, the Flag should be hoisted out from the building towards the pole, union first.)

8. **When the Flag is displayed in a manner other than by being flown from a staff,** it should be displayed flat, whether indoors or out. When displayed either horizontally or vertically against a wall, the union should be uppermost and to the Flag's own right, i. e., to the observer's left. When displayed in a window it should be displayed the same way, that is, with the union or blue field to the left of the observer in the street. When festoons, rosettes, or drapings are desired, bunting of blue, white, and red should be used, but never the Flag.

9. **When displayed over the middle of the street,** the Flag should be suspended vertically with the union to the north in and east and west street or to the east in a north and south street.

10. **When used on a speaker's platform, the Flag,** if displayed flat, should be displayed above and behind the speaker. If flown from a staff it should be in the position of honor, at the speaker's right. It should never be used to cover the speaker's desk nor to drape over the front of the platform.

11. **When used in connection with the unveiling of a statue or monument,** the Flag should form a distinctive feature during the ceremony, but the Flag itself should never be used as the covering for the statue.

12. **When flown at half-staff,** the Flag should be hoisted to the peak for an instant and then lowered to the half-staff position; but before lowering the Flag for the day it should be raised again to the peak. By half-staff is meant hauling

down the Flag to one-half the distance between the top and the bottom of the staff. If local conditions require, divergence from this position is permissible. On Memorial Day, May 30th, the Flag is displayed at half-staff from sunrise until noon and at full staff from noon until sunset; for the Nation lives and the Flag is the symbol of the living Nation.

13. **Flags flown from fixed staffs** are placed at half-staff to indicate mourning. When the Flag is displayed on a small staff, as when carried in a parade, mourning is indicated by attaching two streamers of black crepe to the spear head, allowing the streamers to fall naturally. Crepe is used on the flagstaff only by order of the President.

14. **When the Flag is displayed in the body of the church,** it should be from a staff placed in the position of honor at the congregation's right as they face the clergyman. The service flag, the State flag or other flag should be at the left of the congregation. In the chancel or on the platform, the Flag of the United States of America should be placed at the clergyman's right as he faces the congregation and the other flags at his left.

15. **When the Flag is in such a condition that it is no longer a fitting emblem for display,** it should not be cast aside or used in any way that might be viewed as disrespectful to the National colors, but should be destroyed as a whole privately, preferably by burning or by some other method in harmony with the reverence and respect we owe to the emblem representing our Country.

CAUTIONS

1. Do not permit disrespect to be shown to the Flag of the United States of America.

2. Do not dip the Flag of the United States of America to any person or any thing. The regimental color, State flag, organization or institutional flag will render this honor.

3. Do not display the Flag with the union down except as a signal of distress.

4. Do not place any other flag or pennant above or, if on the same level, to the right of the Flag of the United States of America.

5. Do not let the Flag touch the ground or the floor, or trail in the water.

6. Do not place any object or emblem of any kind on or above the Flag of the United States of America.

7. Do not use the Flag as drapery in any form whatsoever. Use bunting of blue, white, and red.

8. Do not fasten the Flag in such manner as will permit it to be easily torn.

9. Do not drape the Flag over the hood, top, sides or back of a vehicle, or of a railway train or boat. When the Flag is displayed on a motor car, the staff should be affixed firmly to the chassis, or clamped to the radiator cap.

10. Do not display the Flag on a float in a parade except from a staff.

11. Do not use the Flag as a covering for a ceiling.

12. Do not carry the Flag flat or horizontally, but always aloft and free.

13. Do not use the Flag as a portion of a costume or of an athletic uniform. Do not embroider it upon cushions or handkerchiefs nor print it on paper napkins or boxes.

14. Do not put lettering of any kind upon the Flag.

15. Do not use the Flag in any form of advertising nor fasten an advertising sign to a pole from which the Flag is flown.

16. Do not display, use or store the Flag in such a manner as will permit it to be easily soiled or damaged.

PLEDGE TO THE FLAG

In pledging allegiance to the Flag of the United States of America, the approved practice in schools, which is suitable also for civilian adults, is as follows:

Standing with the right hand over the heart, all repeat together the following pledge:

"I pledge allegiance to the Flag of the United States of America and to the Republic for which it stands, one Nation, indivisible, with liberty and justice for all."

At the words "to the Flag," the right hand is extended, palm upward, toward the Flag and this position is held until the end, when the hand, after the words, "Justice for all," drops to the side.

However, civilian adults will always show full respect to the Flag, when the pledge is being given, by merely standing at attention, men removing the headdress. Persons in uniform should render the right hand salute.

THE FLAG OF NEW JERSEY

The flag of the State of New Jersey was adopted in 1896 and its form specified in the following words: "The state flag shall be of buff color, having in the center thereof the arms of the state properly blazoned thereon." This brief description suggests a wealth of historical lore that makes the flag a very real symbol of New Jersey's past and a subject of lively interest to every patriotic citizen.

The buff field of the flag retains the color of the field of the flag used by the New Jersey colonial troops, and with the blue of the escutcheon preserves the memory of the blue and buff uniforms prescribed by Washington for the New Jersey regiments in the Revolution.

The arms are those specified in 1776 for the Great Seal of the state, which the first legislature had ordered. They show three plows, indicative of the agricultural pursuits of the state at that time, on a blue field, with Ceres, the goddess of fertility, and Liberty as supporters. Ceres, bearing her horn of plenty, is on the observer's right, and Liberty, bearing the symbolic liberty cap upon a staff, is opposite her. The crest is a horse's head set upon a helmet and wreath.

My Classmates

~~Alice McElroy~~
Marie Reilly
Joan Needles
Irene Sekas

George Townsend
Ted Baer
Bruce Weston 44-45
Nancy Allen
Jimmie Kruger
Miles Butler 44-45
Clifford Booth 44-45
Helen J. Schutz
Mary Adkisson
Chuck Abbott Esq.
Marietta Weston
Billy Marlin 45
Shirley Conover
Marie Dutch
Virginia Anne Vaughn
Martha Sanker
Jane C. Thompson

My Classmates

MEMORIES OF SCHOOL DAYS

My Teachers

Lillian B. Henry

Elizabeth S. Hayes

Romaine Webb

Marion E. Carter

Jane G. Steelman

Dorothy M. Budd

Grace E. Riddle

B. Josephine Berry

Ralph E. Frazier

Nancy B. Senn

Armenia Townsend